Nectar of Nondual Truth

CONTENTS

10 Vedanta 101
by SRV Staff
In this issue's installment of Vedanta 101, the subject of purifying the mind with initial practices is taken up, particularly prior to intensifying one's sadhana.

12 Universal Daoism & Advaita Vedanta
by Lam FuHo
Every religion has two faces: a conventional side followed by the masses, and a deeply profound essential expression. In Daoism this is seen as the difference between Heavenly Daoism, and Universal Daoism. The latter enjoys close proximity with Advaita.

16 Chochmah
by Rabbi Rami Shapiro
In the Kabala it is written: "You may call intelligence by the name 'Mother.'" Thus, in every religion, if one looks closely enough, Mother Wisdom stands revealed.

18 Threading The Needle
by Annapurna Sarada
A profound inspection of Sankhya Yoga's Threefold Sorrows of Existence and Eight Great Accomplishments lends this article depth, as it reveals both the challenges of remaining on the spiritual path and the secrets of single-minded focus on the Chosen Ideal.

25 On The Haj
by Nur Al-Jerrahi/Lex Hixon
This testament to a sensitive soul's pilgrimage to Mecca is a rare, personal telling that uncovers some of the hidden secrets of Islam, revealing its abiding substance and its universal status.

30 The Blue Sky Of Enlightened Mind
by Jamgon Kongtrul Rinpoche
Stripped of all projections, conceptions, and overlays, the mind, which ordinarily clouds and covers divine Reality, turns clear and radiant once all superimpositions are rendered transparent.

32 The Search For Everlasting Bliss
by Swami Brahmeshananda
Happiness, joy, elation, bliss — although these are all different degrees of one, alluring quality, the measure of the final one, called *Ananda* by the luminaries of India, puts an end to any and all further desires in life.

35 Nonseparation & Its Practice
by Babaji Bob Kindler
The Yogas of Ananya and Abhyasa, well known to all yogic practitioners, are explored here, along with their salient qualities that, when coalesced into one practice, elevate and accelerate both the level and ability of those who succeed at mastering them.

41 Teachings From The Katho Upanisad
by Swami Aseshananda
In a rare recorded class by this late, illumined swami of the Ramakrishna Order, several obscure secrets of the Katho Upanisad are brought to light, revealing that the purpose of life is to transcend the illusion of death.

44 Brahmacharya In The Modern Age
by Brother Tadrupa
The unseen virtues of moderation and abstinence find beneficial expression in this article, supporting all who seek to store up both physical and subtle energy for purposes of dharmic life and Self-Realization.

47 Interfaith Reflections
by Reverend Chris von Lobedon
In all religious faiths and traditions there are singular and exemplary people who hold fast to the elevated Ideal of the harmony of all religions, and do so despite the obvious differences and variations in both paths and personalities. To find such souls is to find God residing in human beings, and to be able to call and see them as spiritual brothers and sisters — as true friends and helpmates in the work of unification.

"For, though Atman is everywhere, it is in the forests of hushed sanctuary, not in the wilderness of human activity, it is abiding on the far-reaching view of the mountain of spirituality, not dwelling at the foothills of endless problems and confusions, it is in the depths of the ocean of Bliss, not in the sea of suffering-ridden samsara, that we find our true Self."

Publisher's Page

Sarada Ramakrishna Vivekananda – SRV Associations
"Setting the feet of humanity on the path of Universal Truth."

Notes on an Advaitic Journal

At the basis of Advaita as the philosophy of Shankara and his gurus, there is Advaita as experience. Advaita as experience represents that supreme place where all diversity merges in its Essence. It is not combatant or immiscible with qualified or dualistic approaches, but rather provides them their place of consummate arrival. Where actual practice rather than mere book learning is emphasized, where religion, philosophy and spirituality are not separate from one another, where knowledge and love, reason and devotion, are never divorced from each other, there does the truth of authentic nonduality effloresce.

Historically speaking, experiential Advaita originated with the ancient Rishis. Therefore, the Upanisads contain the nondual truths of the Vedas which declare: idam mahabhutam anantam aparam vijnanaghana eva, *"This great Being is endless and without limit. It is a mass of indivisible Consciousness only."*

SRV Associations & Universality

The SRV Associations are part of a worldwide movement of spiritual aspirants devoted to the study and practice of Vedanta and Divine Mother Wisdom. The ideals of this ancient pathway to God, exemplified in the lives of Sri Sarada Devi, Sri Ramakrishna and Swami Vivekananda, are the original and eternal perfection of the Soul and its inherent oneness with Reality, the manifesting of divinity in our lives, selfless service of all beings as God, and reverence for the ultimate unity of all sacred traditions. To this end our purpose is to study, worship, and contemplate Truth so that spirituality may flourish. This is the Advaitic way — *"None else but Self, none other than Mother."*

Nectar's Mission — Advaita-Satya-Amritam

In Sanskrit, *amrita*, nectar also means Immortality – and this is, indeed, what we are offering: opportunities to become aware of this Amrita that is our very Essence via the rarefied teachings from Vedanta and the World Religions and Philosophies that appear in each issue of Nectar.

Nectar of Non-Dual Truth is SRV Associations' heartfelt offering of highest Wisdom to the human community. It is the sincerest form of love and service we know to disseminate nondual Truth and teachings which transmit pure knowledge, pure love, and true universality. Through Nectar we are working out SRV's mission of spiritual upliftment and education. Please join us; this is a universal movement.

Keeping Nectar in Print

Nectar is a free magazine that can be ordered in printed form online at www.srv.org, and it can also be viewed online. (play.google.com/books) However, substantial donations are needed every year to maintain this publication in print. Why is this important?

1 – Printed Nectars are best for person to person and organization to organization dissemination of these ennobling teachings that deepen one's own spiritual life and engender knowledge of, acceptance, and reverence for all other paths.

2 – Only printed copies can reach those who do not have access to online viewing, including prison inmates, who are a particular focus of SRV's social seva.

Use the subscription/donation form provided at the back of this issue to send a check or credit card payment to SRV Associations, P.O. Box 1364, Honokaa, HI., 96727, or donate online at www.srv.org. Your donations are tax deductible.

With reverent gratitude, we heartily thank the contributing writers of this issue of Nectar of Nondual Truth, who have so graciously and selflessly shared the wisdom of their respective traditions and practices.

Staff of Nectar of Nondual Truth

Publisher
Sarada Ramakrishna Vivekananda Associations
an Annual Publication
For more information concerning the SRV Associations or Nectar of Nondual Truth please contact:
SRV Associations, PO Box 1364, Honoka'a, HI 96727
Phone: (808) 990-3354
e-mail: srvinfo@srv.org   website: www.srv.org
Nectar Subscription is on a donation basis only

No part of this publication may be reproduced or transmitted in any form without permission from the publisher. Entire contents copyright 2019. All Rights Reserved. ISSN 1531-1414

Editor
Babaji Bob Kindler

Associate Editor
Annapurna Sarada

Production
Lokelani Kindler

Cover Image:
Annapurna Sarada

Acknowledgement
Image of Ramakrishna's Disciples Courtesy of Vedanta Press

800-816-2242

Contributing Writers
Swami Aseshananda
Swami Brahmeshananda
Jamgon Kongtrul Rinpoche
Lam FuHo
Reverend von Lobedon
Rabbi Rami Shapiro
Sheikh Nur al-Jerrahi
Annapurna Sarada
Babaji Bob Kindler
Brother Tadrupa

EDITORIAL

"May peace be unto plants, peace be unto animals, peace be unto mankind, peace be unto ancestors, peace be unto celestials, peace be unto gods & goddesses, peace be unto luminaries, peace be unto the Trinity, may peace be unto Peace."

In order to dwell within and enjoy the bliss of Nonduality, Peace of Mind is required. This abiding Peace is predicated upon the attainment of equanimity and contentment, and both of those are dependant upon fulfilling one's desires in the dharma. But there is one onerous presence that can, almost effortlessly, undo the practitioner's crucial spiritual practice and spoil a sincere aspirant's bid for Peace leading to Enlightenment, and that is the insinuation of work, or action. According to Swami Vivekananda, "Work is the midday sun that is burning the very vitals of humanity. It is necessary for a time, but in the end is a morbid dream." This is even more true in today's humming multiple marketplaces and office buildings, whose teeming masses rush, like a raging springtime river in spate, to gain everything that the world can offer — all of it empty and unfulfilling in the end. Activity can never bring about liberation either, but is more often the cause for bondage of the soul to matter and nature. As Shankara has reminded us, "Moksha can never be gained by thousands of asanas, or by hundreds and thousands of breathing exercises, nor by millions of acts; nor does wealth and progeny bring it."

Yet all these are what the worldly-minded and the pseudo-spiritual hanker after on earth. Some of these may end up with temporary happiness, but none of them will get Peace of Mind — what to speak of the "Peace that passeth all understanding." The always honest, ever truthful Upanisads state: "That One, the Eternal among noneternal things, the Intelligence of the most intelligent ones, who though ever one, fulfills the desires of the many — the wise ones realize That One as dwelling in their own Self. To them belongs Peace, and to none else. Om Peace, Peace, Peace."

The stillness of a Zen Monastery, the placid silence of an isolated and unpopulated tropical island, the quietude of a remote Himalayan pilgrimage retreat, the breathless Air of Heights far above the low-lying valleys of human activity that Lord Buddha mentioned — all of these are actually available to peace-seeking souls here on earth. But where is peace in the workplace? Peace at home? Peace in society? Peace among religions? They all depend upon the peace of mind of the individual first.

Withdrawing from society for forty days and forty nights like Jesus did, or sitting under a Bo tree for 49 days like Lord Buddha, or taking refuge on a mountain for 30 days out of every year as Mohammed did — these types of austerities are far beyond the capabilities of most beings today. Those who already hear the voice of the Divine early on in life do not retire from the company of men because they need to, but because they relish peace. So they are examples. Seeing them, we are to sit for a hour twice a day, and go on retreat away from family (and phones) and activities, as Sri Ramakrishna advised. Only then will that "still small voice" expand, increasing to the sound of AUM — the real Voice of Brahman — so that peace can descend without obstacles and interruptions. For, though Atman is everywhere, it is in the forests of hushed sanctuary, not in the wilderness of human activity, it is abiding on the far-reaching view of the mountain of spirituality, not dwelling at the foothills of endless problems and confusions, it is in the depths of the ocean of Bliss, not in the sea of suffering-ridden samsara, that we find that true Self. As Ramprasad Sen, the ecstatic lover of Mother Kali, sings to humanity: "Sail with me! Come sail with me! Release the moorings that bind you to the harbor of mundane human convention. Unfurl the sail of 'Tara, Tara Tara,' and sail smoothly across the sea of relativity."

In this precious issue of Nectar of Nondual Truth are to be found words of wisdom coming from all-peaceful quarters, from human beings who have settled the score with the world of constant variances. They suggest to us a variety of paths to Peace, and we must set foot upon one of them. For, as Vivekananda has stated to us, here in the West, "It is good to be born in a religion, but one should not die there." From hearing about religion, to practicing it, on to realizing its message, such is the "winsome way" to all things positive and beneficial. All else is only the "wending way," and embodied souls have seen far too much of that time-twisted trail with no final destination. It is time to consummate, to equalize, to withdraw the thought projections of the mind at the end of every day — whether it is busy or not — and rest firmly in birthless, deathless, timeless, spaceless Peace.

Om Peace, Peace, Peace

Babaji Bob Kindler

NECTAR OF ADVAITIC INSTRUCTION

Questions from Our Readers

The copious flow of wisdom thrives best in the atmosphere of holy company, and expresses itself most astutely and cogently via the mechanism of questions on the nature of Reality. But Reality, once realized, is simple. It is the world-bewitching, mind-perplexing maya that requires apt queries.

"I have read about the two modes of Maya, collective or cosmic (samasti) and also the individual aspect (vyasti). I want to make sure I have it. Basically when we look at appearances in Maya as a whole or aggregate, this is samasti. Math seems like a good place for examples. Suppose you had a "pie" cut into sixths. One could think of the "pie" as a 6/6 i.e., six slices of 1/6th a pie where one mentally tends to the idea that there are 6 individual slices. This would be vyasti-Maya. But one could also say that there is 1 pie thinking of it as a single unit without parts which would be samasti-Maya. Is this a good example?"

Yes. It is also good to look at cosmic and collective as two segments as well, though here they are being explained as one. Cosmic would equate to the Trinity, and Cosmic Mind, and the collective would then be all the beings in the subtle worlds (like the ancestors). Then, the individuals could represent earthly beings. Another word, vyapi, explains the All-Pervasive that holds both samasti and vyasti in It.

"I would further add that since our individual experience with the Universe of Name and Form (Maya), being dependent upon our individual sankalpic process, samskaras, and how the mind assigns name and form to generate understanding resulting in "I am experiencing 'X' or this experience means 'Y', that the experiences themselves are illusory in a very tangible and obvious way. Is the 'pie' six 1/6ths or a whole? If I look back on a past experience and call it a happy period five years after the event, but 10 years after that I call it a "dream" and "play" in ignorance and suffering, what was the reality? It is unfigurable in a sense. So, not only is the Absolute in association with Maya causing the apparent division between the Paramatman and Jivatman, i.e. between the personal and individual soul, this process is also going on in trickle down process from the whole cosmic projection, to celestial realms/worlds, to nations, to organizations, to smaller groups of beings, down to the individual. Is this a good analysis and understanding of the modes of Maya?"

Yes, very good; your further explanation takes in and infers all that I wrote above.

"In regards to Holy Mother's teaching that peace of mind is first and foremost to all things, how does one reconcile the strong emotions that avatars like Christ have displayed? An example is when Christ enters the temple and commerce is occurring within the holy walls and He throws a table in response to the situation. This could lead one to believe that Christ had lost his peace of mind and demonstrated anger. Also, when Christ was brought news that Lazarus had died and He wept? How to explain this correctly?"

The visitation and possession of Peace of Mind does not preclude empathy and compassion that the illumined souls always hold for those who suffer. In fact, it includes them fully. Sri Ramakrishna also wept at the death of His nephew, though he was over it in a day. Holy Mother wept at the loss of Yogin, and also when Sri Ramakrishna left the body. Being human, in the embodied condition, is difficult. We ought to look more at worldly people diverting their attention with possessions, pleasures, and relationships, and puzzle over that. People will never be able to avoid the death of their own body and of their loved ones, and the suffering that ensues as a result.

We are behind the curtain of maya here on earth, and no one can see clearly through it. Great souls penetrate it and take a glimpse, sometimes a long look (samadhi), but maya falls over the Eye, and the eyes, immediately thereafter. I have taught some about the Curtain of Nescience. Doubt, fear, and ignorance are all there. Where is clarity? When Jesus sees priests allowing money-lending in the temple, His anger mounts in clarity and He delivers them a lesson. But do they learn? Usually not. One must increase one's sensitivity, and prepare oneself for the needful and the inevitable — and do it early on. Things will go better, or at least far less worse, if one does.

"If an Avatar is a divine manifestation of the 'One without a second,' and does not come into the body with karma of his/her own, how does one explain the negativities that various Avatars go through? For example, Sri Ramakrishna with throat cancer, Christ with crucifixion, Holy Mother with her sufferings, etc?"

Everyone who takes on a body must suffer the karma that comes with it. This is called prarabdha karma, or present karma. Ordinary beings carry past karma and do works unconsciously that amass future karma. These two karmas are absent in the illumined soul.

So, the present karma is the only karma that is operative in the luminary, and their selfless actions bring them near to the karmas of others, willingly. Called "vicarious atonement" in Christianity, it is something like that in Vedanta as well, with the differences being that the sins, karmas, and sufferings are not imminently real, and can be neutralized — not just by surrendering the ego to the Ishtam, but by "cutting oneself in the image of God" via spiritual disciplines and thereby attaining liberation, not just salvation.

Thus, the sufferings we see in these great souls are taken on purposefully by them. Holy Mother used to say, seeing the rashes that came up on Her skin, or the malaria that sometimes attended Her, *"I do not know where they come from, or any other suffering that comes to me. I never committed any sins in the past."*

"We hear about the principle of 'letting go' so that we don't allow the mind to brood and lose peace. My impression is that this idea of letting go has gained popularity, particularly among the hatha yoga crowd and the like. I see my friends following this idea, but it seems that it may be coming from a state of tamas rather than from sattva. Could you expand more on this concept and describe how to do it with the correct orientation?"

You are so correct in your evaluation of this precept of "letting go." The phrase, "Let go and let God," among the Christians, is better than this new age version. The new age version is loosely connected to the psycho-therapy communities of this day and time, as if letting go of one's negatives thoughts, alone, will somehow enable one to actually realize their higher ones! People are always wishing for an easy way to profound and intense levels of awareness, and ever leaning towards weakness as they do. There is no substitute for hard work, i.e., sadhana, and this fact remains the same whether in the field of action or the realm of thought."

"Do some Vedantic philosophers divide Maya into three modes — individual, collective, and cosmic — rather than only two, where samasti includes both collective or cosmic? It would seem that doing so would not really add any understanding to the doctrine of Maya other than perhaps calling out the fact that one can envelope a series of wholes into greater and greater (or more abstract) wholes. For instance you could take all the worlds and akashas and form them into the most abstract or general space known as 'the universe of name and form' and this would be the cosmic outlook. So the main point of samasti is that something is being regarded as an aggregate or whole and this is one of the ways Maya is superimposed over Brahman. Is this good thinking?"

I brought up the third division to you, so it is no surprise to see you entertaining it here. I prefer the three divisions system, having studied the Shaivaite Spandas and 12 higher tattvas, for it goes farther in explaining much more about what we do not experience with the gross senses, and what is beyond them.

Also, three divisions fits with the three gunas, like we were just talking about at class, a sort of gunic cycle that pertains to whole lifetimes. It would stand to reason, then, that beings coming into form with rajas predominant were probably living in the subtle body of a demigod previously. They evince such energy and use it for domination and gathering up wealth, etc., but do not possess refinements such as compassion and the like. Then there are beings born who are very godlike and noble, as also ones that are slothful, meek, and violent.

"Can you further elaborate on why samasti-Maya goes with the ancestor realm and lower heaven? Does it also go with the realm of the gods and goddesses? In your answer, could you explain it in relation to Sw. Nikhilananda's language and discussion about how something is being viewed as a whole or collective from the samasti-standpoint of looking at Maya? My question is prompted by the fact that the ancestors and gods and goddesses are still individual beings, residing in a different world from this realm. While the realm is subtle, it does not make sense how we are looking at 'a number of trees from the collective standpoint and describe them as a wood,' as Sw. Nikhilananda explains it. Thus, it is not quite clear to me how they are under the influence or aligned with samasti-Maya. If you mean the ancestors and a collective form lower heaven, then I can see this. Please further elaborate."

For better understanding of vyasti and samasti you can place the word "mind" where maya is listed. Cosmic Mind, Collective Mind, and Individual Mind make up relative consciousness, from causal to subtle to gross. Ishvara, Trinity, Mahat equate to Cosmic; everything from the gods on down to the ancestors relates to the collective. Human minds are the individuals. I have quite a few charts on this type of viewing that are often shown at class.

"It is my understanding that according to saucha, one should always be truthful when it comes to known facts (although I have heard that it is acceptable to tell a "white-lie" in the situation where the truth will cause more harm than the "white-lie"). Can you please expand on this and inform me if my understanding is in the right light?"

I think you are talking about the yama, satya, here, and not the niyama, saucha. Presuming that to be true, I will answer accordingly.

Conventional upbringing, society, and religion all have this idea that to tell a lie is wrong. That is because they have never had a beneficial lie told to them, and also have seldom avoided telling a harmful truth. Holy Mother told us to never tell a harmful truth. Sri Krishna told the asuras a lie at the end of one of the cosmic cycles so as to protect good beings from what evil beings would have done to them otherwise.

So, many things are not black and white, but often gray. The important thing is what mode or level of consciousness these acts and words are performed in. Even a killing, if done in the right frame of mind, can amount to good and avoid karma. The wise knowers of Reality may say and do things from a higher mind perspective, to protect others from harm. For them, there is no negative result, and if there is, they will take it on and dissolve it straightaway.

Of course, when one is starting off on the path, it is best to follow the tradition to the letter. Once strength has been gained, and higher understanding has come, a certain freedom descends that allows for the vision of higher good to be accomplished by the sensitive soul. As Swamiji said, it may be necessary to compromise with the world at times, but never compromise the Truth. And so we keep our ideals high and intact, but not narrow and rigid.

"What is the recommended method for returning vrittis to their source? In your Raja Yoga lesson 9 it discusses the importance of separating the self and Self, gaining one of the last two States of Mind (ekagra/niruddha), and being in sattva. But what is the action one should take when, say, a negative thought surfaces? One could 'let it go' or dismiss it, but that seems to be close to suppression. One could consciously observe the thought, and treat it with a nonreactive and discriminating mind. This seems better, especially if one is in sattva. What should be the daily practice here? Thank you for your insight."

Both of what you suggest here are methods that can work, and success in them depends upon the nature and abilities of the practitioner. To take the mind off of a negativity is not suppression if there is a positive thought (like Ishtam or mantra) to replace it. As Holy Mother told us, *"When you are about to do or think something that is not right or good, stop and say to yourself, 'What would Mother think?'"*

So bring in your power. Soon those thoughts will not even "think" of coming up.

"Are there limitations on what the human mind can project in the gross world, or any 'rules' according to which the end result of the evolution process must operate? If so, can we think of these as (or connect them to) the scientific laws of Physics?"

Only with metaphysics will one begin to have success connecting what is thought of on this earth as the "matter only schools," and the finer levels of consciousness that attend upon the lokas, or realms of finer awareness. Metaphysics will also have to give way thereafter, lending a path to a brighter understanding that breaches the present void between it and pure intelligence. So long as this "creation" is not thought of as a projection of the mind and then followed up by the realization that the projection is not real, the human mind of today will remain two giant steps away from fuller comprehension. Otherwise, the mind of today is so stunted under the "matter only" and "matter is real" ways of thinking.

"In Raja Yoga, Swamiji describes dhyana and samadhi as follows: 'When the mind has been trained to remain fixed on a certain internal or external object, there comes to it the power of flowing in an unbroken current, as it were, towards that object. This state is called dhyana. When one has so intensified the power of dhyana as to be able to reject the external part of perception and meditate only on the internal part, the meaning, that state is called samadhi.' This is a little difficult to understand intellectually. Could you comment and/or expand on what Swamiji is describing?"

Well, my first thought is how kind Swamiji is being towards the attainment of samadhi, and even towards meditation. For most beings it is not that easy at all. But he is giving us the benefit of the doubt, and also simplifying Yoga so that newbies can begin to practice it.

As to the dynamics of his words, after intense practice has been engaged in, the seeker finally succeeds in doing away with the outer object, i.e., not holding it nor averse to it, and can actually focus on the realm of the mind — as if it were more real than the realm of objects. This is seeing more towards the source, or origin, of all things in nature. The advantage is not just being able to call oneself a meditator, but further, to be able to perceive the worlds as projections of the mind in maya. This will lead to freedom rather than just to meditating on matter and mind for the rest of one's life. Of course, he is most likely referring to all that leads in towards Ishvara when he cites "the internal part." Right perspective around objects can confer a lower samadhi on the mind, but higher principles like Ishvara can transport the mind into a nondual state via inspiration. By studying these Yoga lessons you will acquire more comprehension of all the levels and mysteries of Yoga per se. Keep it up.

"When it comes to situations in the world where nature is being destroyed (ex. forest fires) or animals are being killed (due to fires, human actions, etc.) what is the best way to think and handle these situations? I have a tendency to focus on the essence of the things which remain unaffected and the practice of sending peace out in all directions which helps me to maintain peace of mind and thereby not focusing on the horrible acts in this world by themselves. Other people are more affected by these situations of animals suffering or nature being destroyed, so when they focus on the essence of these things they attain some level of balanced mind, but still feel a very strong sense of sadness that the animals are experiencing suffering. Are there other methods of pacifying the mind such that deep emotions don't sway the mind from balance to such an extent?"

Not so much other methods, but ultimatums. Nothing should affect one's peace of mind; the wise have already agreed on that. In the case of nature (plants, insects, and animals), there is not any fully developed consciousness present there, so whereas the loss is unfortunate, it in no way measures up to the loss of human life in a human form or birth. There is great potential in the human form (even if many of them are still acting like animals). In that life-form God can be realized, and when it is, all of nature vibrates better and benefits — including plants, animals, and insects. Of course, even the death of human beings, occurring by the millions, constantly, leaves no mark, stain, or loss on Brahman. That is the real point, and the most beautiful Truth.

"I understand that Saguna Brahman is Brahman with attributes. Does this mean that Ishvara is the highest aspect of Saguna Brahman that the mind can conceive of before being immersed in Nirguna Brahman?"

Yes, that is the idea, and the Truth. Thus, Ishvara is also an idea, a form, but It is the highest and best — like getting to the Father through the Son. Of course, one has to go deeper and actually see and realize the Father.

"If the gross world is the projection of the collective consciousness, is the dream state a projection of individual consciousness?"

The individual is an essential increment of the collective. Just as it has in it the full scope of the Atman, it also has the full scope of the collective and cosmic as well — just as a drop of water has the full essence of water in it. As for projections, the origin of all of that is in the cosmic mind, or Mahat. From there it trickles out and down to the collective (samasti), then to the individual (vyasti). All the while, it has the entirety (vyapi) within it.

So, It is a mass of Consciousness alone, and it takes the Great Mind to begin to portion it out, so to speak. We see that the Great Mind, Mahat, is no more seen or even heard of much here on earth, and even with the ancestors in subtler lokas it is overlooked as well. Every individual is taken up with its own projection and knows little of anything else. Only the selfless, or those who follow that trend, will come to know it. Those rare ones see everything as a projection of mind, i.e., a mass sankalpa. How many of those are there in any given time, or age? Precious few. The rest adhere to matter and its seeming transformations. To see the Mahat is to begin to see into the truth of nonorigin — that Reality has no change in It whatsoever.

"I've been thinking about a teaching of yours where you mention how it is best to just sit for meditation without any expectations (for a good meditation, vision of God, etc.) and I just want to make sure my understanding is correct. The reason why we should not have any expectations is because when there are expectations there is duality, and the purpose for meditation is to realize one's nondual Self. Thus, one should sit without any expectations, such that they can return all vrittis to their source and transcend the mind (the very mind that would harbor expectations). Is this correct?"

Yes, from the standpoint of practice, this is best. From the perspective of who you really are, Atman, this same experience is transferred by not even thinking you are meditating, or that there is even an act of meditation — or anyone to meditate upon other than your own Self. The wandering Avadhut, while walking, all of a sudden just sits down and enters a spontaneously concentrated inner state; he never planned to "meditate."

"I also believe that what is inferred in your teaching is that sitting for meditation for meditation's sake does not mean that one just 'gives in' and does not try to control the mind. For if this was true I can see this attitude simply resulting in a continuance of tamasic/rajasic mind. So, one must sit for meditation simply because this is what we do (as aspirants/devotees) and then work to control the mind during meditation, without having any expectations of whether you were successful or not at controlling the mind. Is this understanding in the right light?"

Yes. But this is a high ideal. One may be able to achieve it at times, but it is very difficult to do so when the gunas shift, and one has to move amidst worldly atmospheres, etc. Thus, the practices pertaining to early and intermediate stages have to be observed, like yamas and niyamas, even though we know and keep in mind the absolute and true nature of states and things.

"What's the difference between the waking and dreaming states that leads souls to act of their own volition in the waking state, then act according to what the mind dictates in the dreaming state? This may only be an observation (and maybe not even an accurate one), and I am just wondering if there is any significance, or if this fits into the teachings somehow? Is everything perceived, observed in both the waking/dreaming projections? If so, why the difference between the two?"

As you may remember, Gaudapada stated that there is no real difference between the waking and dreaming states of human awareness; the very same things happen in one that occur in the other, the only obvious difference being that they "happen" on gross and subtle planes. This should be noted rather than compared. If the principle of mental projection (sankalpa) is accepted, and the course of life subjected to observation in meditation, not only will the tendencies of confusion (moha) and violence (himsa) be tempered, the soul will also get a glimpse of the Light that underlies everything and thus be able to give up dreaming and projecting and come to rest in the "Peace that passeth all understanding." This puts one beyond the intellectual frame of reference. To put it in another way, it is nondifference, not difference, that leads the soul to its highest realization.

"A broader question has come up in the mind in different contexts. While reading the chapter on prana in Raja Yoga, I was wondering more specifically about pranayama. If one goes through one of the prescribed breathing exercises without bringing much consciousness to it, can one still affect the awakening of Kundalini? Is it essential to bring consciousness about with the flow of prana (via breathing) in order for the awakening to happen? I know that in some of these western hatha 'yoga' classes you can find instructors leading the class through breathing exercises, but doing so in total absence of awareness of the teachings of the dharma."

It is always best and more effective to bring consciousness, or one's awareness, to bear, and focused, prior to starting into any method of aspiration. To consult a preceptor, guru, or at least a mentor early on, is also wise, for then the method or methods — all of which have defects in them — will show up such dangers and the seeker can avoid them, deftly. For the illumined, pranayama is not necessary. For the adept practitioner, the mind has already been controlled, so again, pranayama may not be needed. In both these cases the Kundalini has been raised already by innate intelligence — Her favorite quality. It is only in the case of intermediate and beginner types of seekers that these preliminary exercises are recommended. Here too, and more so, the guidance of an adept will help practices bear fruit quicker and without mistakes. For, it is highly unlikely that authentic Mother Shakti Power will awaken, or remain in the mind's awareness, if the prana is not consciously awakened and purified as well. Then it has to be utilized properly. Guru, dharma, sangha — we wish that more beings would use these mainstays of true spiritual life and practice.

"Can we think of Jesus' healing miracles in terms of Prana? A story came to mind, that of the woman who was bleeding for 12 years and thought if only she could touch Jesus' cloak that her physical body would be healed. She did, and it was. When it happened, Jesus was said to feel the flow of power from Him. Was that Prana? (This also reminds me of touching the Guru's feet). Can this be extended to all of Jesus' healings?"

We can and should think of healing powers, and miracles, as the tricks of prana. Miracle-mongering/mystery-mongering is a danger in true spiritual life, and has almost ruined the Christianity of the day. The negative effects of occult powers have long been known in India. Sri Ramakrishna mentioned them as "crow droppings alongside the road." Even Jesus did not like them, and used them sparingly, "only for the disbelievers."

Still, healing comes from different levels of prana, and is used beneficially or detrimentally by beings of various abilities, higher and lower. In an illumined soul the power of refined prana has been sublimated and turned into ojas and tejas. This is higher, better. All one needs to do is somehow touch the body or garments of such a being and positive benefits get transferred. When two people touch one another lovingly, their purity gets shared between them. This is good, but middling. When anyone tries to heal or impress using their own personal power — depending on the quality of the soul who is the agent — this is lower because the ego is involved.

For the actual mechanics of how prana works you can tune into all the classes I give to find those periods spent on the subject. There are several very good charts on prana too. Basically, Vedantists concentrate on psychic prana more than on physical prana, for by mastery of the former the latter automatically comes under control. This is why the illumined souls never have to do asana. Their psychic prana is mastered, and so their mental posture purifies all that has to do with the body. For instance, yogis seldom get sick, are mostly free of disease. Even if they do contract something (which is often for purposes of helping others) they control that disease from the mind as well.

"I have also been thinking of the vritti of sleep, analyzing how the mind is upon awakening, and how to control the vritti of sleep. So far, I have noticed that by employing utsaha and dhariya (from the 5 Aids of Steadiness of Mind) I have been able to transition from the sleep state to the waking state with a relatively clear mind. This analysis has also lead me to further investigate how the vritti of sleep comes over the mind. Thus far, I have been able to consciously (at least I believe this to be the case) notice this vritti coming over the mind and I liken it to a cloth being pulled over a table. The table is the mind and the cloth is the vritti of sleep. Now, the next step in the process is to figure out how to prevent the cloth from being pulled over the table. This is where I am stuck. Can you elaborate on how one goes about controlling the vritti of sleep?"

Change that cloth that you are laying over the table unknowingly in sleep to clear plastic. Then you can see through it. That is, sleep is natural to the human body/mind mechanism, but haziness and slothfulness are not — or should not be considered to be. So wake up the mind. Imagine what it is like to be spiritually awake in the waking state. Attain that (mastering the "A" of AUM), then do the same in the dreaming state, i.e., awaken in your dreams too. Know Thyself. You are presently the sleeper and the dreamer; now be the ever-awake one, in all states of your own being. Consciousness is your territory. Claim it!

"**Additionally, I have been thinking that controlling the vritti of sleep is an important key in progressing to the next level in my meditation practice. I've continued to increase my intensity in the form of walking through curtains or catching wind currents to raise the mind 'up' (as you have advised), but I have a feeling that what I am encountering is somewhat related to this vritti of sleep. The reason why I think that the vritti of sleep is involved in what I am facing is because I believe that I am running up against the curtain of nescience. Is the vritti of sleep related to the curtain of nescience? If so, can you please explicate on their relationship and how, if they are related, the aspirant can use the control of the vritti of sleep to pierce through the curtain of nescience.**"

Yes, sleep and this curtain are related, and support one another. Where the curtain of nescience differs is that it operates more at the collective level, whereas sleep is an individual phenomena, as it were. So you need to divorce yourself from collective consciousness (detachment, as mentioned by you above), and you are doing so by practicing spiritual disciplines that most other beings know nothing about and are not interested in. This is why you have to make conscious efforts to transcend the ancestor realm and its pervasive and insidious (and usually unknown) influence upon you (samskaras and desires, etc). Do not worry about feelings, sentiments, suffering, and all that. Get yourself free first, then turn to help others. As our Great Master has stated, *"When a man gains freedom he is not attached to wife, children, and relatives anymore; he only retains compassion for them."*

On a very fundamental level, sleep has merely become a habit. Like every other attachment in life, people feel it is necessary. It is, but only to a point, i.e., resting the body and senses. But why do they never consider the ever-awake state as a necessity? The world is mostly water, but there is land. In the same way, the lives of most beings are mainly sleep — on the physical, emotional, mental, psychological, philosophical, and spiritual levels — but there is pure, conscious Awareness. Seekers of Truth want to find that singular Territory and abide in it always.

"**Could you give the Vedanta definition of demoniac?**"

In two parts, the first (as in the Sanskrit word, moha, deluded) would be that anyone who is unaware of their true nature as Atman, and is instead attached to the physical world and its objects to the exclusion of the existence of God/Brahman, that being would be considered mentally imbalanced and thus dangerous to their self and to others — even if such beings were acting as if they were good, moral persons. In other words, if the ego is in control of the human being rather than God/Atman, then such beings are under the unhealthy influence of demonic forces.

A second definition follows the Sanskrit word "asura" more closely. The asuras are demoniacal, since their nature is warlike, and they are always and ever looking to increase their power, lands, and possessions for selfish reasons. Still, their natures are not completely evil, as in the case of the Christian Devil (even he did not start off evil) and is mixed with some goodness and some intelligence. Again, however, the ego is strong in these beings, whose sense of righteousness and superiority does not allow them to be peaceful or humble in the face of others.

"**Are there connotations attached to the definition of occult? (e.g., are occult 'ways' negative in some way?) Maybe I just** need a definition here too?"

Yes, the Ashta Bala Siddhas, or eight occult powers, have a goodly amount of negativity assigned to them. This is so, in part, due to their attraction for the soul who wants to gain name, fame, gain, and all other lower attainments, using them. It must also be said that the quality of one's consciousness comes into play here as well, with some beings able to resist this temptation, others not able to do so and thus ruining themselves with power, and still others who can use the powers sparingly for a higher purpose and give them up immediately thereafter so as not to be tainted by their possession. Of course we are aware, in this day and age, of the paltry and insignificant level of the occult such as preoccupation with things like levitation, clairvoyance, and metaphysical dabblings into crystals, tarot cards, astrology, and the like. But in India, the occult powers were always of a higher level. Even still, the seers warn people away from acquiring or using them — even if for a so-called "higher" purpose.

In short, it is telling how few people go for acquiring higher wisdom and how many seek the occult. Sensationalism and mystery-mongering are a few signs of the presence of the occult in the shallow human mind.

"This question is about the extent to which the consciousness that one brings to one's actions impacts the resultant karma. For example, if through a direct result of one's actions some harm to another being occurs, but maybe unknowingly or unintentionally by the responsible person, do they develop less karma than one who consciously, or due to negligence, harms another?"

Usually and in most cases the amount and intensity of karma remains the same, act to act, accordingly. For instance, those boys who set off the smoke bomb recently that killed so many forms of life and displaced people from their homes have a karma to pay, no doubt. But Lightning does the same, and worse, each year. With more consciousness dwelling in the human entity, more awareness in the sentient being, comes karma in keeping with any given act upon that soul.

Now, if that recent fire was caused by some kids who started it unknowingly, would not the karma be the same according to its effects? We live in a puritanical society where sin is taken as real, and judgement and punishment are the only way to recompense it. But no one has ever passed judgement on that particular bolt of lightning that was responsible for thousands of acres of lost forestlands, and many deaths. No one even sued that bolt, or brought it into court to pay a fine and sent it to prison. Karma is just a law, but it is an unforgiving one. It metes out its own justice without a speck of malice or remorse. To be careful of what one does and how one acts is the best policy, then, but even then one cannot escape the inexorable laws of karma.

The same is true of "random acts of kindness." Random means unconscious. So no real good comes of them, at least not of a conscious and lasting kind. To insert consciousness into each and every equation, and to be ready to forebear both the positive and negative effects that may come from them, is then the best mode of operation for the embodied soul on this gross plane of consciousness.

"Relatedly, can one render an act classified by conventional society as negative, not negative, depending on the mindset?"

Yes, the world of higher mind and nondual perspectives is full of instances of beings who are beyond the pale of mundane human convention in their thoughts and actions, and who bring about higher good through unconventional means and modes. And in fact, it is healthy to strive for such purer atmospheres and abide in them, for otherwise the mind gets stymied by the world of causes and effects and its consciousness begins to coagulate around inferior ways of perception. To try and be an original thinker has always been the way of the wise, and least in the early stages of transcendental leanings and attainments. Later in spiritual life the wonder of "not-thinking" can mature.

"There is a sentence in Lesson 1 of Raja Yoga that states: 'Since knowledge is a vritti — a wave in the mind — all knowledge is objective.' I don't understand how A implies B. Why does it follow that knowledge is objective because it is a wave?"

This does not concern a wave in the sense of quantum physics, but instead a "vritti," an intelligent vibration of consciousness. And there is a witness or onlooker to such vibrations; That is you, looking upon your own thoughts. That transcendent Being is called the Eternal Subject; everything else is an object to It. And so we must learn to detach from the infernal objects so as to realize the Eternal Subject — our Self, Atman.

"I'm having a hard time accepting some of what seem like dualistic teachings in our tradition that at 'face value' seem to differ little from Christianity. For example, the Master's story of the cat playing with the kitten and mouse really seems like it makes the Lord into a punisher and rewarder, depending on one's level of submission/surrender. How is this any different from saying God punishes sinners and rewards saints?"

You may be confusing God/The Lord with karma, here. In the Gita, Sri Krishna states that the Lord does not take notice of the transgressions of anyone, that nature does all that. Karma is in nature, nature in karma. The kitten and mouse have both found their way into nature. It pampers one, pains the other.

Nondualism is supreme, especially so long as it is mature, but we nevertheless bow to qualified nondualism and dualism, both, which are very rich, and an important part of living life dharmically. Further, it is not that Christianity's teachings about sin (avidya) and damnation (samsara) are all so wrong; it is more that, over time, they became the accent rather than the watchtower. Where is the god in the universe that judges? It is Ishvara, the Trinity, and the gods and goddesses associated with them. They are all maya, being in form, but they represent higher maya (Mahamaya). This higher maya is to be secured by reverence, worship, and propitiation through bhakti sadhana. All of the above mentioned are strong powers, and not to be thrown away blithely due to some as yet underdeveloped sense of nonduality that may or may not mature in the future.

Questions, observations and insights regarding problems in spiritual life or the issues of the day may be directed to Nectar's editorial staff at srvinfo@srv.org and will be duly addressed in succeeding issues.

◆ SRV Staff

VEDANTA 101
One Should Not Intensify an Impure Mind

"A man named Podo once entered a dilapidated temple infested with bats and decided to be the priest there. At dusk he blew the conch shell and the surprised people began to gather. When the people entered, they saw the priest dressed in improper garb, and they also noticed that the temple was unswept and there was no deity on the altar. Then they told him: 'You have not prepared yourself by initial practices and purifications. You must first clean and consecrate the altar, then bathe and dress properly, and then install the deity with the proper rites and mantrams. You have only blown the conch shell prematurely, which amounts to nothing. A loud noise is all that has happened.'"   Sri Ramakrishna

The purpose of purification via spiritual disciplines like meditation, study of scripture, worship, and the like, is to make the mind ready to perceive its own already perfect Essence. This true nature that Vedanta calls *Atman*, or what is termed Buddha Nature or *Svarupa* in other Indian philosophies, is present and all-pervasive, even here on the physical plane, but is covered up by the clouds (see article on page 30) of mundane thought and action; the depths of peace are covered by the surface of restlessness. When these effects are smoothed out by purificatory practices, called *sadhana*, then thought and action themselves become effective means for expressing the divinity within oneself.

Inspecting these few teachings on proper orientation will lead one to desist from thinking thoughts and performing acts based in slothfulness (*tamas*) and restlessness (*rajas*) and begin striving for balance in thought, word, and deed. Nor will normal balance, called *sattva*, be enough to gain the peace and bliss of Enlightenment, for thinking and acting in this penultimate condition will only cause the mind to form impressions of happiness and pleasure, and it is well known to advanced practitioners (*sadhikas*) that both of these qualities only lead, in cyclic fashion, back to experiences of sorrow and pain.

Who Would Strengthen Weakness?

When the sincere aspirant has come to recognize the power for transformation of mind that spiritual disciplines possess, the mode of practice should shift for the better. Intensifying the specialized practices indicated and transmitted by the guru is wise only if the mind is ready to implement them. Otherwise the impurities already in place in the fourfold mind (*manas*), thoughts (*chitta*), intellect (*buddhi*), and ego (*ahamkara*) will intensify along with the increased power, and major errors along the path will occur — errors that will result in the worst mistake of all — quitting the path, practice, and preceptor.

Simple analogies may help in understanding this simultaneously complex but straightforward *dharma* teaching. If one were to place a piece of ripe fruit onto a pile of moldy fruit, the result would be disasterous. In similar fashion, taking a ripe teaching from the spiritual preceptor, like the nondual truth of *Ayamatma Brahman* (this Self is Brahman), and introducing it into a mind that is still filled with uncertainty and bad thinking habits (*klistha vrittis*), will only increase negative tendencies, skew the desired interpretation, and waylay right understanding. This is why Sri Ramakrishna warned that it is not good to give the nondual truths to worldly householders or beginning sadhikas. They must perform the purificatory practices pertinent to their present position. For, who would give a sharp knife to a child, or gift a rare jewel to a baby?

Wise Before One's Time

Novices and beginners have one great quality going for them. They have the energy and verve necessary to propel themselves along the early stages of the path. With the guidance of a good teacher progress can be made, but the present of inexperience puts them at risk. They may take on too much too soon, filling the body/mind mechanism with practices that are still beyond them and subjecting the mind to the expansion of its consciousness prior to the arrival of maturity of outlook. Right perspective, then, is a key principle to be observed in early spiritual life, and is to be maintained carefully by the intermediate and advanced seeker as well.

Indian Buddhism provides good insight and instruction along the trajectory of this important *dharma* teaching. The chart opposite shows that the first facet of practice of the eightfold path is perfect view, or right perspective (*samyag-dristi*). Unfortunately, it usually matures at a later stage of the practitioner's progress, but it would be best to have it in place early on. And all other important facets of the path will also operate correctly and smoothly if right orientation is learned and implemented at the outset of one's initial self-effort.

The end result of careful and well-guided progress along the spiritual path is what both Vedantists and Buddhists call *khyati*. It is clarity of mind. The Upanisads state that "....*pure water poured into pure water remains the same.*" As a nondual teaching this is fine indeed. But so much of impurity (*ashuddha*) is present in the individual and collective mind in this day and time (*kali yuga*). One would not pour swamp water into drinking water only for the reason of increasing the amount. Purity of mind, *chit shuddhi*, is one of the most coveted attributes of the sages and seers. Evil thoughts, banal thoughts, gross thoughts, mundane thoughts, worldly thoughts, even mere intellectual thoughts — if Brahman is not placed first before them — are brackish water into which no wise aspirant will place the higher teachings of spiritual life....what to speak of then intensifying their content with well-intentioned but under-informed knowledge and effort.

The Four Noble Truths and the Eightfold Path

"Recognition of the Four Noble Truths equals Spiritual Awakening; Nonrecognition equals Ignorance."

I The Truth of the Existence of Suffering — Dukha

Sorrow — Lamentation — Pain — Grief — Despair

(The Five Aggregates)

II The Truth of the Origin of Suffering — Samudaya
(Due to Craving/Desire)

III The Truth of the Cessation of Suffering — Nirodha
(Due to cessation of Craving/Desire)

IV The 8-fold Path leading to the Cessation of Suffering — Ashtangika-marga

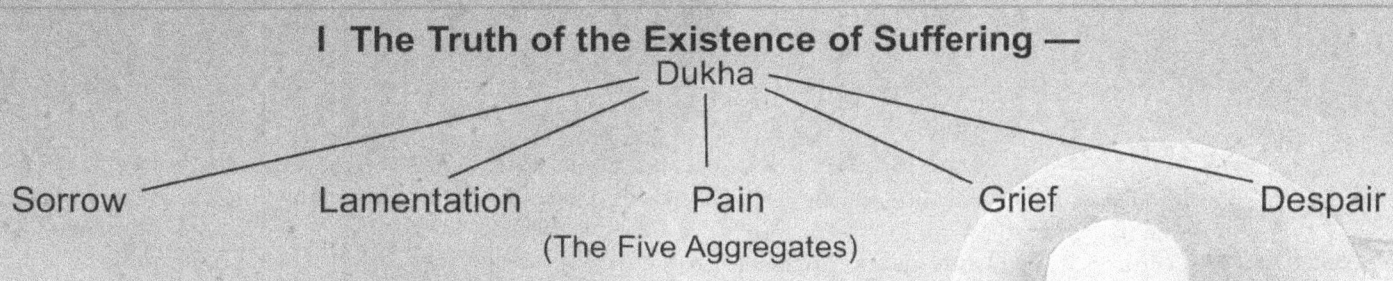

Stage 3 (Prajna) — Wisdom & Insight	1 Samyag-dristi — Perfect View	Direct insight into the Dharmakaya. Knowledge of the unity of all existence
	2 Samyak-samkalpa — Perfect Resolve	The stilling of all mental projections. Mature renunciation. Goodwill to all fellow beings. Absence of the desire to do harm
Stage 1 (Shila) — Discipline & Morality	Samyak-vak — Perfect Speech	Knowing the limitations of speech. Refraining from lying, gossip, slander, etc.
	Samyak-karmanta — Perfect Conduct	Abstention from profit-oriented work. Conformity with ethics and morality
	Samyak-ajiva — Perfect Livelihood	Avoidance of detrimental occupations. Realization of the eternal nature of dharma
	Samyak-vyayama — Perfect Effort	Freedom from conflicting intentions. Accrual of good karma, avoiding bad karma
Stage 2 (Samadhi) — Concentration & Meditation	Samyak-smriti — Perfect Mindfulness	Freedom from vexation/brooding. Sensitivity in regard to body, mind, thought
	Samyak-samadhi — Perfect Concentration	Freedom from opinions. Acquisition of the Four Absorptions of Mind

ADVAITA-SATYA-AMRITAM 11

◆ Lam FuHo

SIMILARITIES BETWEEN UNIVERSAL DAOISM & ADVAITA VEDANTA
Highlighting Similarities — As in Building a Bridge

天道 *tiandao*, or Heavenly Daoism, also called 一貫道 *yiguandao*, is at its deep core a Chinese school of Universalism. Preferably, Universal Daoism is an appropriate alternative name. It is philosophically all-inclusive and its focus is primarily on scriptural studies of Chinese Mahayana Buddhism, philosophical Daoism, and Confucianism. Christian scriptures are studied in lesser quantity; nonetheless, salvation, self-surrender, repentance, and worship for the Highest, are incorporated. Overall, Universal Daoism aims at liberating every single person from suffering. By gaining wisdom and higher Knowledge, good actions and vegetarian diet, devotion and worship, mantra and mudra practice, concentration and surrendering the ego, remembrance of Highest and mastery, and letting go of our lower self, eventually we realize the Dao, the Highest Truth, and our Real Self 真人 *zhenren*. In Advaita Vedanta also exists the idea of universal salvation and universal freedom. "*Swamiji wanted Sarvamukti, a realized liberation for all; not just jivanmukti or Videha mukti, signifying freedom for the individual or escape from embodied states. The reason is clear. If even one remains in bondage and suffers, then all will, for all are in One, and the One is present in all…*"

Universal Daoism recognizes 張天然 Zhang Tianran, born (1889-1947) as its main male founder. A contemporary of Swami Vivekananda (1863-1902), both devoted their life in the spread of universal peace, harmony between religions, and Higher Wisdom. Followers of Universal Daoism and Advaita Vedantists are Universalists, although the former should become more aware of it. Universal Daoism, at the same time, includes and transcends religion. In Advaita Vedanta, "*Oneness of existence does not mean numerical oneness, but rather comprehension of indivisibility. It is all-inclusiveness rather than 'this, not that.' You will find a place for all things in Brahman. Sri Krishna referred to it in the Bhagavad Gita: 'What is unreal never really exists, what is real never ceases to be.'*"

一貫道 *yiguandao* derives its name from the way a string goes through coins and connects them all (Chinese coins have holes and were kept together through a string). *Yiguandao* is the One Path which goes through and connects all religions. At the same time transcending religion to spirituality, which is Non-Duality, it is called the Dao, or Its Unmanifest name 無極 *wuji* — in short, Unlimited. There is a similar saying in Advaita Vedanta: "*the thread that runs through a string of pearls.*"

Spiritual Disciplines in Daoism

Universal Daoism emphasizes scriptural self-study and spiritual self-effort; eagerness to know Truth, higher Knowledge, and wisdom. Rituals are limited to their essence. *Qigung* and various kinds of breathing exercises are only suitable to those who have a qualified teacher as exemplar, and live pure and tranquil lives. Otherwise, unsupervised practice could result in mental imbalance and physical ailments. As in Raja Yoga, psychic control and possible occult powers may lead a man astray. The path of psychic control and subtle energy practices are suitable to only a few. Nevertheless, spiritual aspirants should keep their bodies healthy through safe physical exercises. Sri Ramakrishna stated: "*People of small intellect seek occult power, but the genuine devotee does not want anything except His Lotus Feet.*" In other words, Universal Daoism mainly is a knowledge type of spiritual Path (type of *Jnana Yoga*) suited for people with intellectual tendencies. By reading sacred knowledge and wisdom, doing good actions in society (similar to *Karma Yoga*), and through closely following the universal principles of 仁 *ren* Benevolence, 義 *yi* Righteousness, 禮 *li* Courtesy, 智 *zhi* Wisdom, and 信 *xin* Trustworthiness, one creates merit. Merit is believed to be necessary to lift ourselves to higher consciousness. Similarly, "*Atmajnana – Knowledge means realization of your real Self.*" Then as well, "*Jnana, knowledge of Brahman/Atman/Self, even if only based upon an intellectual or indirect understanding, leads to transcendence from both virtue and vice and all other pairs of opposites.*"

Divine Daoist Deities

Saints, sages, and various forms of deities from mainly the Daoist and Buddhist pantheon are included in Universal Daoism. Outer acts of reverence are done through kowtow, which is kneeling and touching the ground with one's forehead. More important is inner reverence, where one's heart should fully concentrate and have an attitude of devotion. Kowtow, aforementioned devotional practices, and mantra recitation, together, are very similar to *Bhakti Yoga*. Also, the initiated are given a mantra, mudra, and point between the eyes to concentrate on as means of practice.

Swami Vivekananda has stated that "*It is not God who created man, but man who created God's Image by way of concept. But when conscious of Atman there is no distinction.*" Similarly, in Universal Daoism, it views seemingly different religions as diverse expressions of the One, The Ultimate. Different needs, customs, cultures and historical background, may express in different religions, but the source is One. This we may call 萬法歸一 *wan fa gui yi*, meaning the "*innumerable methods return to the One.*" Similarly, "*God Itself can be one and many.*" The *Upanisads* state, "*I am ever One, but I become many.*" If beings could but see the truth of Oneness, even just in this one area called "religion," how much closer to harmony and peaceful human relations we all would be. "*It is a rare individual who can bridge the gaps in conventional religious outlook and sow seeds of har-*

> "In the concept of 無為 wuwei we find that it does nothing intentional and yet nothing is left undone. It accepts all in easy non-preference. It lets everything just be, taking its own direction naturally in perfect balance and harmony with the greater whole."

mony leading to the realization of the intrinsic unity of all paths…"

"The broad-minded soul who is open to other pathways to God enriches the mind considerably with uncommon and beneficial knowledge that is quite often missing in one's religion of birth of choice."

"Ekam sat viprah bahudha vedanti" – that Truth is one and sages call it by various names and that all paths lead to the same goal – is the consummate devotee and much beloved of God."

"One essential element of Universality is intrinsic inter-connectedness. Unity is underlying everything, but everything in the universe is inherently unified by nature of its being connected with all other things."

The Natural State of Daoism and Vedanta

In the concept of 無為 wuwei we find that it does nothing intentional and yet nothing is left undone. It accepts all in easy non-preference. It lets everything just be, taking its own direction naturally in perfect balance and harmony with the greater whole. Manifestation of the Dao, creation and transition of all living things are all a spontaneous process. In addition, 一生二，二生三，三生萬物 or yi sheng er, er sheng san, san sheng wan wu, meaning "The Dao is One, the One becomes two, two becomes three, three becomes manifold." In Advaita Vedanta, "The manifold has come from the One alone, the Relative from the Absolute." And, "It is not proper or correct to call the Divine Mother by the title Prakriti (nature), as some do, since She is Brahman, though sometimes in a dynamic mode. Prakriti is insentient; Mother, All-sentience. Sri Krishna emphasizes this in the Bhagavad Gita: 'Some assign to me the appellation of Creator. But I do nothing. My mere presence (as Consciousness) causes Prakriti to manifest all the many things in creation; I stand back as the ever-watchful transcendent Observer."

The concept of 逍遙自在 xiaoyao zizai in Zhuangzi means seemingly free and at leisure, but in fact it lets the Dao run its own course, totally naturally and spontaneously. It is wasted effort to go against It. The sage only acts in accord with the Dao. It is the Dao at work, the individual merely expresses It. From Advaita Vedanta we hear: "Only the illumined beings have "colorless" karma, however, for their works are devoid of any motive or selfish reason."

The Removal of Suffering

The Goal of Universal Daoism is to be free from suffering, from cycles of existence, i.e., liberation. It is ultimately being in Bliss 極樂 jile and identifying with 一點明光 Yi dian ming guang, or one point of Light, as our True Self. One should recognize this Light at the time of death and remember Maitreya Buddha, who is the center of worship. We are to know that we are the future Buddha Himself. We are Immortal, Unborn, and Undying. Swami Aseshananda calls this jivanmukti. "You have come here to attain freedom. Freedom from old age, disease, and death. Realize the Atman, and that you are not the body. Presently you think yourself to be the psycho/physical being. That means you are a wave. But when you become illumined you will realize that 'I am the ocean,' no birth, no death, noncausality. Real nature is unembodied, unfettered – unbound Spirit. God as Nirguna Brahman – God without attributes; God as impersonal, undifferentiated, universal, and timeless, as well as changeless. Furthermore, "Amritattva – immortality. If immortality comes you will have no-body; in other words, all Spirit. The body is limitation. Mind is constantly changing. But unlimited Consciousness will come when you attain Nirvikalpa Samadhi."

Lead Us from Lower to Higher Truth

What is more, in Universal Daoism distinction is emphasized between 教 jiao ordinary religion and 道 dao Highest Truth, or Non-Duality. 道是無處不在 Dao shi wu chu bu zai, 無時不在 wu shi bu zai, that is, the Dao is at any place and at any time. It is right in front of our eyes. Statues, symbols, and temples are only representations of the Ultimate. People live in the Dao, but they are not aware of It. Advanced in spiritual practice, transcending religion towards the Dao, one should detach from imageries and strive perceiving the Dao all around us in daily life. It is the same way in Advaita Vedanta: "Brahman and the world unite and become one. This is "seeing God everywhere and happens only after one successfully spiritualizes everyday life." As well as…."Deifying all of existence. Deification of the world is only possible when one becomes illumined. After illumination comes compassion. Atman is subtlest of the subtle and the greatest of the great. It is much like space – indivisible."

Furthermore, Swami Vivekananda stated: "It is good to be born in a church, [or a temple, a mosque, a synagogue, etc.], but do not die there. One must grow up spiritually and get out of the constricting, soul-killing confines of the religious establishment and become a jivanmukta, a 'free-while-living' soul who has transcended all barriers of race, caste, creed, nationality, religion and become a truly universal human being." And further, "…to attain the lofty state of jivanmukti we need to, as the basic minimum requirement, incorporate in our lives the fundamentals of all religions, such as love, truth, honesty, compassion, nonviolence, fellow-feeling, the spirit of selfless service of others, and not embrace vile fundamentalism."

> 無生老母 *wu sheng lao mao* is The Unborn Mother, also called 無極母 *wuji mu*, or Infinite Mother. She is represented on the altar behind Maitreya Buddha as a flame, the fire of Wisdom, often accompanied by the Chinese characters 無極 *wuji*. We children should always remember our True Nature and yearn for union with Mother.

Concentration and Purification

Besides scriptural study, devotion, and doing good actions in society, concentration practice is as follows: Concentrate at the One point between the two eyes. This point is called the 玄關 *xuanguan* or Gate to the Unknowable. Close the eyelids about 70% and keep 30% open. Repeat the Maitreya mantra silently. Hold the given mudra at chest height close the heart. Sit or kneel with the spine erect. The One point of concentration, mantra, and mudra together are called the three treasures 三寶 *sanbao*. By preference, exercise this each morning and evening, even when calling for help of the Divine during abrupt difficult circumstances, or when encountering frightening images. This practice should concentrate, clear, and purify the mind from rising undesirable thoughts. Thus, this practice resembles *Mantra Yoga* and 'make thine eye single'. In Vedanta, *"The mantra acts on the subconscious mind to remove impurities there. God's Name has this power and ability."* Further, Holy Mother teaches: *"The true Self is ever-pure, but is only recognized when the mind is purified."* Mental purity is the capacity to give one's whole mind and being to God/Self, to not be distracted by any other thing or concept. This purity, in its highest state, is the transcendence of duality and abidance in the Self.

According to 清靜經 *Qing Jing jing*, or Classic of Clarity and Stillness, when desires are absent, then one becomes clear, pure, still, and tranquil. Comparably, the Sri Sarada Vijnanagita states: *"This time the Great Master has shown an easy path; therefore it will be possible for all to realize God. One becomes spiritually awakened by continuously contemplating God. But you can become illumined right now if you become desireless."*

In Daoism, 無極 *wuji*, often is translated as the Ultimate, Boundless, Infinite, or Limitless, for describing the Highest Truth, which is ultimately Indescribable. Identical in Advaita Vedanta is the truth of the Limitless: *"We, the disciples of Sri Ramakrishna, only know this much: never try to limit God. Infinite are his moods and aspects. He is beyond the reach of mind and intellect. And yet, if one earnestly prays to Him, He becomes attainable to the pure mind."*

The Mindful Heart

Harmony between scriptural study and devotion is emphasized in Universal Daoism or, in other words, balance between intellect and emotion. The view is, we are all children of Mother. We may cry tears for worldly affairs, but how many people shed tears for Mother? 無生老母 *wu sheng lao mao* is The Unborn Mother, also called 無極母 *wuji mu*, or Infinite Mother. She is represented on the altar behind Maitreya Buddha as a flame, the fire of Wisdom, often accompanied by the Chinese characters 無極 *wuji*. We children should always remember our True Nature and yearn for union with Mother.

This is very similar to Mother Kali or Sri Durga, the Divine Mother of the Universe in India. Babaji Bob Kindler has written: *"Ultimately, She is realized as the essence of limitless Consciousness — infinite, indivisible, all-pervading, and absolute. The Twenty-Four Aspects of Mother Kali, then, represent in book form an attempt to remind humanity of their divine parentage, of their divine nature, of their source of origin. It is hoped that those who are still asleep to this supreme verity called the Divine Mother of the Universe will have their inherent spirituality awakened..."* Also, from Swami Sivananda (of the Ramakrishna Order): *"Everything depends upon the will of Mother. Knowing that the Mother is ever merciful, continue to call on Her. Let the Mother keep you in whatever state She pleases. In this way, eventually, you will have unmixed bliss and uninterrupted peace."* Swami Vivekananda has stated, *"There must be harmony between Bhakti and Jnanam: "Faith is a wonderful insight, and can save, but there is a danger in it of breeding fanaticism barring further progress. Jnanam, wisdom, is all right, but there is the danger of its becoming dry intellectualism. Love is great and noble, but it may die away in meaningless sentimentalism. A harmony of all these is the thing required."*

Concentrate on the Soul, Less on the Body

借假修真 *jie jia xiu zhen*, means borrowing the body to attain the Real. Comparably, in Advaita Vedanta, one is not the body: *"The Jnani must not try to preserve the body, nor even wish to do so. Always discriminate. Always think that this body is only an inert instrument, and the self-contained Purusha within is your real nature."* And Sri Sarada Devi states: *"Even this body, the identification of the self with the body, must go. It is the body alone that changes, the Atman remains the same."* And She further states: *"Everything – husband, wife, even the body – is only illusory. What is the body, my darling? It is nothing but three pounds of ash when it is cremated. Why so much vanity about it?"*

Once, one of my Universal Daoist teachers told me a story: *"People in the past lived peaceful, harmonious, tranquil, simple, healthy, and long lives. The main reason was because in the past people knew their true Original Nature, and they had remembrance of Mother. So they lived on earth as living in a play, like a dream, and eventually they would return to where they came from — completely peaceful, aware, and conscious."* Put in Vedantic terms, we should have *Nityanityavastuviveka* – discrimination between the real and the unreal. In Advaita Vedanta it is said, *"The reason we suffer is that we have fallen asleep to our higher nature and forgotten the real purpose of human existence, the true meaning. The main obstacle to remembrance is the projection of maya mingling always with our own ignorance. If we can play expertly in maya without falling asleep, and thus refrain from becoming a victim of her projections, keeping our mind on the truth of Existence, then we learn to live in God. Such life is in the Atman, which is your true nature."* And, speaking of the Golden Age of *Satya Yuga*: "*This truth, combined with a unique and sensitive reverence for all of life based upon the five types of yajnas, or sacrifices, caused life to go on as it was generally intended – in peace and harmony. Subsequently, people were more calm, thus more reflective on the facts and truths of existence. Rancor and truculence were therefore practically nonexistent, and harmony and happiness permeated the society.*"

Concluding Declarations

In this article I have highlighted similarities as in building a bridge of peace, trust, and mutual respect between two universal wisdom traditions. It is unity through diversity. Each individual follows his and her own path of preference, peaceful and in harmony with others. Most people with faith on one religion only might also aspire to be universalists in this regard. Each individual is unique, and we must let people have religious freedom.

Concerning globalization and cross-cultural exchange nowadays, Universalism is, in my opinion, the suitable solution and philosophical axiom for peaceful co-existence between people of diverse religious, cultural, and socio-political backgrounds. Universalism is all-inclusive in nature. Another way to implement it for people with dual tendencies could be to first follow a single path diligently, and later adopt a second path which complements the former. The rule would be to respect similarities and accept differences.

In this article, then, Advaita Vedanta has intellectually, logically, systematically, and greatly clarified the heart of Universal Daoism. Intellectually speaking, all paths of interest should be safely studied. Some spiritual aspirants, however, expect a total and complete picture of Truth. Our time to read and study all the holy scriptures available from major world religions and spiritual paths is limited, and so the task is unrealistic. To avoid surface eclecticism, i.e. taking bits and pieces without prior comprehensive study, syncretism might mature. Universalism as a theological and philosophical concept with syncretism as its application, will make the two mutually inclusive.

We must recognize essence and understand the true meaning of texts in each religion or spiritual path. We must notice the universal inner values, applicable to all human beings. Some traditions, e.g. Tibetan Buddhist and Daoist traditions, absorb the useful elements suited to their cultural background and needs after profound comprehension. The non-useful elements to one may be of great aid to another. Nothing positive should be rejected. In this point, Universalism complements syncretism. As Sri Ramakrishna has stated: "*Gather all information and then plunge in. What will a man gain by merely reasoning about the words of the scriptures? Ah, the fools! They reason themselves to death over information about the path. They never take the plunge. What a pity!*"

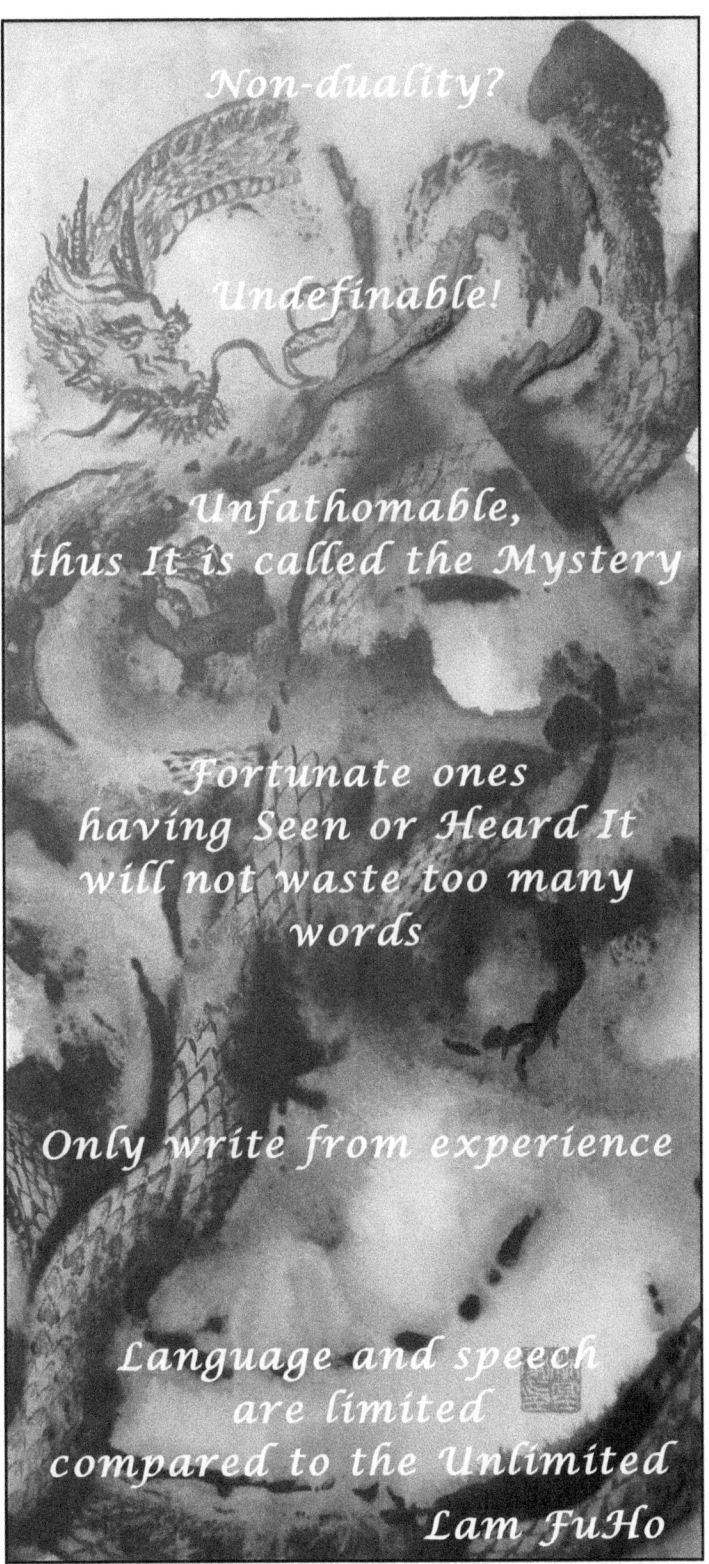

Non-duality?

Undefinable!

Unfathomable, thus It is called the Mystery

Fortunate ones having Seen or Heard It will not waste too many words

Only write from experience

Language and speech are limited compared to the Unlimited

Lam FuHo

Lam FuHo 林富豪 is a Universalist and sinologist. Often called the 'Uomo Universale' for his expressions generally in music, painting, and poetry, he believes the concept of Uomo Universale has similarities with the Daoist concept of self-cultivation — mental and physical self-improvement as well as spiritual practice through the arts. His intellectual interests are in Advaita Vedanta and Christian mysticism. Daily practices are from Daoism and Buddhism.

◆ *Rabbi Rami Shapiro*

Chochmah

Mother Wisdom in Judaism: An Introduction

The fundamental role of Wisdom in religion is undeniable. It should be one of religion's main aims to instill Wisdom, or higher Knowledge, into the minds of embodied beings. Otherwise life — even religious life — tends towards mundanity, or even worse, war and chaos. The Bible puts this very succinctly: "I looked upon all the works that my hands had wrought, and on the labor that I had labored to do; and behold, all was vanity and pursuit of the wind, and there was no profit under the sun. And I turned within myself to behold wisdom, as well as madness and folly. Then I saw that wisdom excelled folly, as far as light excels darkness. Then I invested myself with Her as a raiment of glory, and put Her on my head as a crown of joy." And with the honorable station of Philosophy, as well, it should be no different. Philosophy is not for desire, fame, occupation, debate, or willful argumentation: "Existence is proof of God's existence." It only takes true Wisdom to reveal this. As Swami Vivekananda has stated: "The Divine first becomes knowledge, then, in the second degree, that of will. Though knowledge, being a compound, cannot be the Absolute Itself, it is the nearest approach to It, and higher than will or desire."

Wisdom, *Chochmah* in Hebrew, is the first of God's manifestations and the means by which creation happens. She is, to borrow from the Latin of Baruch Spinoza, both *natura naturans*, the creativity implicit in the very nature of reality, and *natura naturata*, the results of that creativity — creation itself. Or, to borrow from Chinese Taoism, she is *tzu–jan*, that which of itself is so. *Chochmah* is what is, and how what is is what is.

> I am the deep grain of creation, the subtle current of life.
> God fashioned me before all things;
> I am the blueprint of creation.
> I was there from the beginning, before there was a beginning.
> I am independent of time and space, earth and sky.
> I was before depth was conceived,
> before springs bubbled with water,
> before the shaping of mountains and hills,
> before God fashioned the earth and its bounty,
> before the first dust settled on the land.
> When God prepared the heavens,
> I was there.
> When the circle of the earth was etched
> into the face of the deep,
> I was there.
> When the stars and planets soared into their orbit,
> when the deepest oceans found their level
> and the dry land established the shores,
> I was there.
> I stood beside God as firstborn and friend.
> My nature is joy, and I gave God constant delight.
> Now that the world is inhabited, I rejoice in it.
> I will be your true delight if you will heed my teachings.
> (Proverbs 8:21–31)

Chochma "pervades and penetrates" all things (Wisdom of Solomon 7:24). As *natura naturans*, Wisdom is "*intelligent, holy, unique, manifold, subtle, active, incisive, pure, lucid, invulnerable, gracious, keen, irresistible, loyal, trustworthy, all-powerful, all-pervading, and all-penetrating,*" (Wisdom of Solomon 7:22-23 NRSV).

As *natura naturata* Wisdom is —

> the structure of the world and
> the activity of the elements;
> the beginning and end and middle of times,
> the alternations of the solstices and
> the changes of the seasons,
> the cycles of the year and
> the constellations of the stars,
> the natures of animals and
> the tempers of wild animals,
> the powers of spirits and
> the thoughts of human beings,
> the varieties of plants and
> the virtues of roots; ...
> all that is manifest and all that is hidden.
> (Wisdom of Solomon 7: 18–21)

Jewish Wisdom teachings are fundamentally humanistic. One is not asked to worship Wisdom or to follow the commandments of God found in the Hebrew Bible. The goal is simply right action:

> Do not hold back from helping others;
> share what you have without reservation.
> Do not say to the needy:
> Ask me again tomorrow,
> when you can do something today.
> Do not sow seeds of evil nor betray those who trust you.
> Do not quarrel even with those
> that do not have your best interests at heart.
> Do not envy the violent nor imitate them,
> for one who strays from the path of peace
> turns away from all that is holy;
> only the upright are intimate with God.
> The houses of the wicked are condemned,
> but the homes of the just are blessed.
> Do not underestimate the power of association:
> align yourself with scoffers and you will scoff;
> practice humility and you will be appreciated.
> The wise inherit honor, the legacy of the fool is disgrace.
> (Proverbs 3:27–35)

> "There is no need to reference God as the author of Wisdom. There is no sense that these teachings are good and right because God ordains them as such. On the contrary, they are good and right because any wise examination of life will reveal them to be good and right."…. "Wisdom's only desire is to teach you to become wise. Her only frustration is your refusal to listen to her."

Where do these obligations come from? Are they prefaced by, *"Thus spoke the Lord God"*? No. There is no need to reference God as the author of Wisdom. There is no sense that these teachings are good and right because God ordains them as such. On the contrary, they are good and right because any wise examination of life will reveal them to be good and right. There is no focus on observing *mitzvot* (divine commandments), or conforming to ritual norms. Wisdom is gleaned from life experience rather than ritual observance.

How do you become wise?

"*Search for Her and seek Her out, and She will reveal Herself to you. When you lay hold of Her do not let Her go. Take your rest with Her at last, and She will become ecstasy for you.*" (Wisdom of Jesus ben Sirach, 6:27-28 NRSV).

Chochma is not a reluctant guide or a hidden guru. She is not hard to find, nor does she require any austere test to prove you are worthy of her. Rather, she "*stands on the hilltops, on the sidewalks, at the crossroads, at the gateways*" (Proverbs 8:1-11) and calls to you to follow her. Wisdom's only desire is to teach you to become wise. Her only frustration is your refusal to listen to her.

The way of Wisdom is study, observation, and clear perception. What you study, observe, and perceive is Wisdom as well, for she is both the Way to and the Way of. Wisdom "*knows and understands all things,*" (Wisdom of Solomon 9:10) because she is the creative energy through which all things arise. To know her is to know the Way of all things. But you cannot study *Chochma* in the abstract, for there is no abstract with her. You study *Chochma* by studying life and the myriad living beings that comprise life.

The ultimate gift of Wisdom is overcoming the existential sense of alienation Judaism posits as the core human dilemma. In the parable of the Garden of Eden, God sees that humanity, having eaten from the Tree of Knowledge of Good and Evil (essentially the Tree of Duality), has become *achad mimenu* (Genesis 3:22), usually translated as "like one among us." The Hebrew, however, literally means "unique from us," or "one separate from us." Becoming *achad* means that humanity can no longer see itself as a part of the divine whole. Instead, humanity imagines itself to be apart from rather than a part of both God and nature.

Chochmah/Shekhinah

What Albert Einstein called "optical delusion"

A human being is a part of the whole, called by us, "universe," a part limited in time and space. He experiences himself, his thoughts, and feelings, as something separated from the rest, a kind of optical delusion of his consciousness. This delusion is a kind of prison for us, restricting us to our personal desires and to affection for a few persons nearest to us. Our task must be to free ourselves from this prison by widening our circle of compassion to embrace all living creatures and the whole of nature in its beauty.

God expels Adam from the Garden because God fears Adam would eat from the Tree of Life and would in this way be forever locked into this optical delusion.

Chochma is the cure for the disease of *achad* (alienation) and the optical delusion that supports it. Seeing through the illusory duality that is *achad* (imagined alienation from the whole), we awake to *echad*, the unity of all things in, with, and as the nondual Reality Judaism calls God, YHVH, the Happening is all happening. Embracing Wisdom is one way Judaism offers to achieve this goal.

Rabbi Rami Shapiro is an award-winning author, poet, essayist, and educator whose poems have been anthologized in over a dozen volumes, and whose prayers are used in prayer books around the world. Rami received rabbinical ordination from the Hebrew Union College–Jewish Institute of Religion and holds doctoral degrees in both Jewish studies and divinity. A congregational rabbi for 20 years, Rabbi Shapiro currently teaches Religious Studies at Middle Tennessee State University, and directs One River (**www.one-river.org**), a not-for-profit educational foundation devoted to building community through contemplative conversation. Rami writes a regular column for Spirituality and Health Magazine called Roadside Assistance on Your Spiritual Journey. His most recent books are The Sacred Art of Lovingkindness, The Divine Feminine, and Open Secrets from which this essay was adapted. Rabbi Rami can be reached through his website, **www.rabbirami.com**

◆ *Annapurna Sarada*

ThREADING ThE NEEDLE
Overcoming the Web of Karma

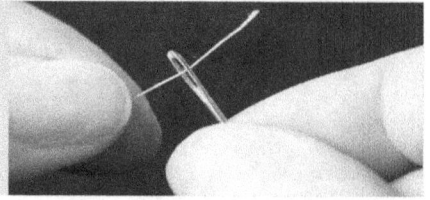

Sri Ramakrishna used the analogy of threading a needle to describe the necessity of making one's mind one-pointed in order to realize God and be Free. If even one fiber is sticking out, the thread will not pass through the eye of the needle. It is a homely teaching with deep ramifications.

What does the needle signify? It is *Maya, Samsara* – living in ignorance of one's true nature and accepting (or reacting to) the world of sense perception as real and true. The thread is one's mind and all it contains. And the fibers that stick out? – these are of different kinds but all hinge on the mind's desire (attachment and aversion) with regard to objects and *karmas* resulting from actions performed self-ishly (i.e., with the sense of "I," "me," and "mine"). As Patanjali, the Father of Yoga has observed: *"Beings suffer bondage to pleasure [and pain] due to performing actions with attraction and aversion to matters they have assumed to be accurate based upon unstable vrittis of the mind"* (sense perceptions, thoughts, reactions, emotions, memory, instinct). Together, these weave a multifaceted web of *karma* within oneself, with others, and with subtle or cosmic forces. To "lick the thread" is to cease creating new *karma*, forbear and transcend existing *karma*, and stand firm against encroachments upon one's spiritual life, which alone is *"the bridge to immortality,"* i.e. realization of one's Self as infinite Existence, Knowledge, and Bliss – needle threaded!

This web of *karma* brings us to the main subject of this article, which is intended to discuss the challenge that many experience early on after choosing a life of *dharma*, a transformative spiritual life. It is a common occurrence that "life" (read: *karma*) in the form of family, friends, work, health, and other events, very often "coincidentally," and repeatedly, asserts itself over a new practitioner's goals for spiritual practice and participation with teacher and spiritual community – holy company. It is initially mystifying and disruptive, and is a grave danger to spiritual success unless one skillfully perseveres.

This challenge has posed itself for as long as there have been spiritual aspirants wanting to dedicate themselves to God and Self-Realization while living in the world. Even those called to monastic life will have to jump this hurdle to enter and continue in holy orders. But the householder, married or single, by virtue of interacting with all aspects of "life," has the greater challenge. Thus, victory is amazing to behold, though rare – the householder yogi or yogini who demonstrates the truth of *"being in the world but not of it."* Sri Ramakrishna also encouraged spiritually-minded householders by comparing a *dharmic* home life to a safe fortress in which to practice spiritual disciplines. Ramprasad Sen, the great mystic poet of Bengal, also affirms, *"You will receive Mother's Wisdom while sitting at home in quiet meditation, disciplined by the responsibility of ordinary life."* Both encouragements to the householder, however, are based upon the assumption that one engages daily in spiritual disciplines – worship, study, and/or meditation, selflessness in action, and spends time in holy company free from worldly influences.

Some say that modern global materialism, with its rampant corporate greed and insensitivity, as well as the ever-elusive search for financial security and happiness dependent on technology, have made things worse in the extreme these days. However, an ever-deepening spiritual life still comes down to a question of priority and determination. If one's priority is constantly shifting with "life," little progress towards lasting peace and freedom will be made. The waves of interference will continue unabated. A disciple of Sri Ramakrishna once wrote to a student who was putting off his spiritual practices for better times, that one would never get a holy bath by standing on the beach waiting for the waves to cease. The good news, however, is that the great teachers have assessed the problem and offered up solutions.

The Three Sufferings

The great sage, Kapila, the father of the Sankhya system compiled several thousand years ago, enumerated Eight Great Accomplishments, *Astadhah Siddhih*. The first three are primary, and refer to overcoming the Three Sufferings: *Adhyatmika* (internal), *Adhibautika* (external), and *Adhidaivika* cosmic,(as shown on the chart, p. 19. This attainment signifies victory over *karmic* influences at all levels of one's being: nothing inside, outside, or from "on high" has the power to avert one from the path of Self-Realization. Studying each of these sufferings in the context of past and future lifetimes illumines the significance of *karma* in each category of suffering. It is also important to grasp that *karma* is not just individual, but also collective – i.e. family, community, nation, with the ancestors, and even with the deities/powers that control/empower the cosmic processes, including one's senses. A story from India's *Itihasa* (sacred, mythological-historical scriptures) explains this symbolically:

A sage had reached the last day of a prolonged austerity that included fasting. The gods of the elements and senses watched breathlessly, realizing that this sage was on the cusp of total control of his senses and mind. If he succeeded, he would no longer be under their control and they would not receive their share of his enjoyments experienced self-ishly (i.e. enjoyment accompanied by the sense of "I," "me," and "mine"). These gods determined to interfere with his vow and state of perfect equipoise. One of the gods then embodied as a wandering holy man and approached the sage just as he was about to end his vowed austerity and partake of food. The "holy man," came to him for alms. The sage willingly gave him some food, thanking God for the opportunity to render service. The next god embodied as an emaciated beggar, to whom the sage joyfully gave all the rest of his food before taking even a crumb. Praising his Chosen Ideal,

> "There is a popular notion that "goals" stand in the way of enlightenment, but this pertains to advanced practitioners working on the most subtle limitations. Without betraying the truth of Nonduality, one can and must engage in spiritual disciplines for purification of the mind with the foreknowledge of the inherent perfection of the Self/Atman."

the sage thought within, "a fast can properly be broken with water." Raising his cup to his lips, he spied a bedraggled and panting "dog" desperately in need of water. Without hesitating to serve God in yet another creature, he gave the water to the dog. The gods then all appeared humbly before the sage, submitting themselves as servants to the Master.

In Sankhya Yoga's list of the Eight Great Accomplishments (p. 20), we see that attaining the removal of the Three Sufferings are the Three Primary Accomplishments. The Five Secondary Accomplishments facilitate their attainment over time when engaged in with sincerity and perseverance. Making progress in these "Five" helps one gain ground in removal of the three sufferings. This, in turn, facilitates greater attainment of the "Five" because one is neutralizing, forbearing, detaching from, and ultimately transcending and/or eliminating the causes of *karmic* occurrences that have previously interfered with establishing a steady, ongoing spiritual life. Along with all this, one is gaining in sustained peace of mind and contentment.

The Four Kinds of Karma

Before continuing with an exploration of the Eight Great Accomplishments, the four basic kinds of *karma* described in Indian philosophy and psychology should be explained in brief. *Karma*, itself, means action as well as its result. Every kind of self-ish action – thought, emotion, speech, actions performed with the senses and with one's limbs – is karma. Their results, whether immediate or delayed, are also *karma*. Actions are conducted with objects: conceptional objects of the mind, one's own body, external objects such as desirable and undesirable insentient things, and also with sentient objects like people and animals. The seeds of delayed results/*karmas* accumulate in the mind (not brain), or subtle body, and sprout in future lifetimes.

This "basket" of stored *karmic* seeds is called past *karma* (*sanchita*). When taking on a new body, a portion of that past *karma* is brought forward (*prarabdha karma*) to be dealt with in one's current lifetime. One's body, gender, family, enemies, close friends, and major life events, for instance, are manifestations of this past *karma* brought forward (now called *prarabdha*). New *karmas* created in this life and stored as seeds for future lifetimes, plus one's store of past *karma* – these are called future *karma* (*agami*). There is another kind of fructifying *karma* that is called kriyamani karma ("kriya" implying spontaneous action), and has been described in current times as "putting out fires." These are often created as people deal unskillfully with the main *karmas* (*prarabdha*) of life, exacerbating and compounding them such that life becomes a ceaseless roller coaster. As long as one takes refuge in "life," seeking respite via the search for pleasure and other distractions, karmas do not get neutralized and peace of mind will not be attained. The significance of all this, again, is that these four kinds of karmas are behind the challenges people face not only in daily life, but especially in maintaining their original intention in spiritual life.

Lord Buddha stated that ignorance is nonrecognition of *karma*. Most people, if they even accept that cause and effect occur in the mind and not just in matter and energy, cannot trace the origins of their *karma*. This is not, however, the most important concern ahead, but rather to for-

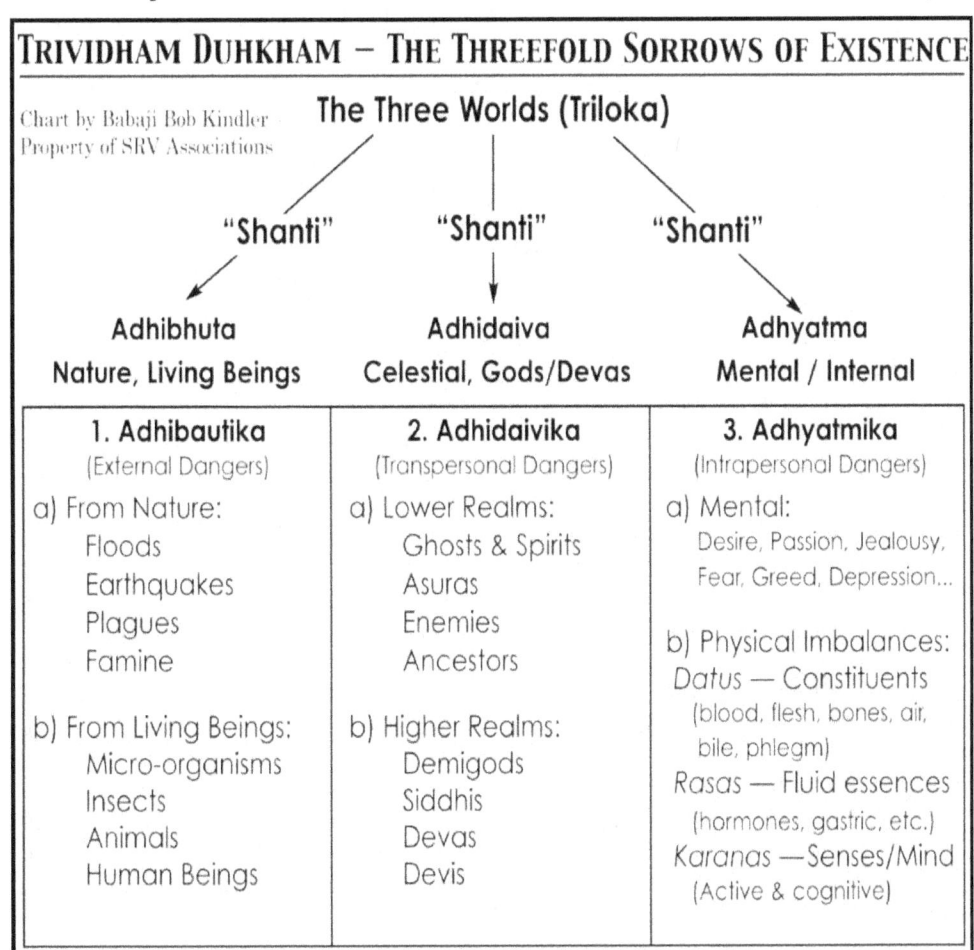

bear the *karmic* events of life and cease making new *karma*. Desire-impelled actions give rise to sufferings across these three divisions of internal, external, and transpersonal/cosmic dangers. Desires for wealth, spouse, children, fame, power, heaven – pleasure of all kinds, here and hereafter – perpetuate the web of *karma* over lifetimes with the objects and persons they were created with. The seeds of *karma* that we plant via self-ish actions must have their effect so long as we remain in cycles of unillumined births. But as the Holy Mother has stated, *"Karma alone is responsible for our misery and happiness. The result of karma is inevitable, but by repeating the name of God you can lessen its intensity. If you were destined to have a wound as wide as a ploughshare, you will get a pinprick at least. Karma's effect can be counteracted greatly by japa and austerities."*

The relative/provisional teachings of *karma* and reincarnation free one from blaming God, gods, society, and others for one's difficulties, and strengthen one's will to engage in spiritual disciplines that lead to Freedom. Lord Vasishtha, in the scripture, *Yoga Vasishtha*, says to the young Sri Ramachandra, *"Current self-effort is greater than past actions* [manifesting as one's *prarabdha karma* now, and potential in the future]." Only *Dharma*, spiritual life and practices intent on purification of mind and Self-Realization, are effective. All other practices will simply immure one in this *karmic* web. In our guilt-prone Western culture we are apt to take all this very personally, but that is not the point, and is also counterproductive. Becoming aware of *karma*, recognizing that it exists only in Nature and not in the Self, will hasten the capacity to forbear, transcend, and destroy *karmas*.

The Five Secondary Accomplishments

The Five Secondary Accomplishments, just like Lord Buddha's Eight-fold Path [see chart on page 11], lead us out of this *karmic* wilderness if we persevere, keeping before our minds the goal or Ideal to be attained (Freedom, Self-Realization, true Peace), "with great love," as the Vedic *rishis* advise. At the beginning and intermediate stages of spiritual life, before one can properly be described as an adept (before peace of mind is one's constant friend and one is deeply intuiting the ever-Free Self within) a goal or Ideal is essential to strive for. There is a popular notion that "goals" stand in the way of enlightenment, but this pertains to advanced practitioners working on the most subtle limitations. Without betraying the truth of Nonduality, one can and must engage in spiritual disciplines for purification of the mind with the foreknowledge of the inherent perfection of the Self/Atman. This is called *Advaita Vedanta Sadhana*.

4) *Dharma:* Pursuing a Spiritual Path – It is both a boon and the mark of prior attainment to encounter a transformative spiritual path early in one's life and contemplate its teachings. Surface or conventional religion is not what is meant by pursuing a spiritual path. Every religion has its conventional or surface aspect wherein many adherents posit their "belief" and observe certain important events. To pursue a spiritual path is to begin to put it into practice in one's life. By following the basic precepts daily, one begins the process of not creating negative *karmas* and cultivating forbearance of the negativities in life.

The Eight Great Accomplishments

The Three Primary Siddhis — Removal of the Three Types of Suffering

1) Adhyatmika — Intrapersonal Suffering
2) Adhibhautika — External Suffering
3) Adhidaivika — Cosmic Suffering

The Five Secondary Siddhis

4) Dharma — Pursuing a Spiritual Path
5) Vidya-shastra — Knowledge of Scripture
6) Svadhyaya — Concentration / Study
7) Sadhu-satsanga — Gaining guru, disciples friends, compatriots
8) Shuddhi — Achieving Self-purification
   Bhuta-shuddhi — Purity of Location
   Kriya-shuddhi — Purity of Action
   Chit-shuddhi — Purity of Mind

---

5) *Vidya-Shastra:* Gaining Knowledge from the Wisdom Scriptures – This refers to higher knowledge, that knowledge by which one realizes the Self/Atman-Brahman as presented in the nondual scriptures. It is knowledge of the Eternal, the Infinite, the Ineffable. With it, one begins to discriminate between the Eternal and the finite, the Unchanging and the changing. Swami Vivekananda has described the importance of this higher knowledge: *"Spiritual knowledge is the only thing that can destroy our miseries forever; any other knowledge satisfies wants only for a time."* And Sri Krishna states in the Bhagavad Gita: *"In all the world, there is no purifier like knowledge. Those perfected in Yoga realize this in due time."*

6) *Svadhyaya:* Study of the Wisdom Scriptures, & *Sadhana*. The distinction between this and the attainment above is that one develops the ability and will to concentrate on the subtle truths of the scriptures. One engraves them upon heart and mind. Spiritual disciplines become a "divine preoccupation" and this destroys one's mistaken identification with the body, the mind with its doubts, desires, fears, and enables one to grasp more and more one's true identity as unconditioned Awareness, transcendent of action and results — the one Self in all.

7) *Sadhu-Satsanga:* Gaining Guru, Disciples, Friends, Compatriots – This describes Holy Company, an indispensable ingredient of spiritual success. Via Holy Company one learns what not to do, as well as what to do to deepen one's spiritual life. By keeping regular company with the *Guru*, one develops discrimination between the Self and the non-Self and detachment from the non-Self. In another charming example, Sri Ramakrishna describes this precious fact of spiritual transmission from teacher to qualified student:

A young person desirous of learning the weaver's trade sought to apprentice himself to a master weaver. Arriving at the master's shop and stating his intent, the weaver told him to bring a 32-strand skein of yarn from a table piled with balls of multi-colored yarns. The youngster had not the slightest idea which one to select and so reached for a random skein. "No," said the master weaver, "That is a 31-strand yarn. Choose that blue one next to it. That's a 32." The apprentice was astonished and thought to himself that learning such a subtle distinction would be impossible. However, after a year of apprenticeship, he too could see the difference, without any direct words of instruction.

Shankara succinctly describes the boon of Holy Company in his stotram, "*Mohamudgara*": "*Through the company of the good arises non-attachment; through non-attachment arises freedom from delusion; through freedom from delusion arises steadfastness; and from steadfastness arises liberation in this life.*"

8) *Shuddhi*: Achieving self-Purification. As a spiritual attainment, self-Purification is the purification of mind that leads to Self-Realization, and certainly signals removal of the Three Sufferings. It is not the cause of Illumination, but rather the removal of what has apparently hidden the Self, like clouds in front of the sun.

The practice phase of self-purification covers three aspects: 1) purity of location and objects, 2) purity of action, and 3) purity of mind. While cultivating the first, one avoids places and objects that cause the mind to focus outwardly via desire and the passions. Instead, one seeks to spend time in those places that are spiritually consecrated or naturally pure, as well as to make one's own home a spiritually charged place via practices such as worship, meditation, and study – not allowing contrary thoughts or activities to enter there.

The second, purity of action, means avoidance of actions that increase desire and other passions which distract one from divine remembrance. The aspirant replaces these activities with those that temper the mind with forbearance, sense control, patience, peace, nonattachment, etc. It is well-known among dedicated spiritual practitioners that worship, contemplation of the teachings, and meditation, inspire the mind and lead to noble actions.

The third, purity of mind, is aided by the first two. As its own focus, though, it requires keeping a watchful eye on the mind, recognizing its moods and modes and how they affect perception and interpretation of inner and external phenomena. In Sankhya, Yoga, and Vedanta philosophical systems, this recognition is facilitated by a teaching called the Three *Gunas*.

These three (*sattva*/balance, *rajas*/activity, *tamas*/darkness-inertia) are present throughout Nature and, most importantly, in the mind. (see "The Three Gunas in Vedic Cosmology," Nectar #30) Holy Mother, Sri Sarada Devi, taught, "*One needs peace of mind first and foremost.*" This initial "peace" is found in a mind that is *sattvic*, balanced, and able to detach from objects, senses, and situations. A mind in this state is more likely to create good *karma*, and if engaged in spiritual practices for a long, long time, becomes poised to attain the transcendent Wisdom necessary for performing actions free of *karma*. By contrast, a *rajasic*, restless mind, which is under the control of desire and passions, creates new *karma* at every turn. A *rajasic* mind sees and interprets everything via ego-centric attachment and aversion. A *tamasic* mind is dull, lazy, often depressed, and negatively brooding. As Sri Krishna warns in the *Bhagavad Gita*, the mind imbued with tamas interprets everything by taking and reacting to one part as if it is the whole, and cannot be convinced otherwise.

Identification with the *gunas* as they rotate through the mind is very dangerous. The Self is *trigunatita*, transcendent of *gunas*, modes, or attributes. Thus, an essential practice of purity of mind is noticing which *guna* is predominant at any time, disidentifying with it, and cultivating the *sattva guna*, balance, via spiritual practice.

The web of *karma* will simply give way under the force of will generated by well-guided, sustained, and sincere *sadhana*, spiritual practice. As light removes darkness, Knowledge of the Self dissolves *karma* and its apparent power to dictate terms. "*The Self is all in all – None else exists.*" Thus, the Peace chants of India end with the benediction to ward off the three kinds of sufferings: "*Om Shanti, Shanti, Shantih – Let Peace prevail in the inner world, the outer world, and on high.*"

Teachings on Trividham Duhkham
(The Three Kinds of Suffering)

1) Adhyatmika — Caused by mind
a) Mental Suffering - cured by internal means:

Suffering	Cure
Passion	Control
Anger	Compassion
Attachment	Self-analysis
Fear	Evolutes / Origins
Jealousy	Generosity
Depression	Nonattachment

b) Physical Suffering - cured by discriminative wisdom, practical regimens, and forbearance

2) Adhibhautika — Caused by other beings
cured by Self-abidance and perseverance

3) Adhidaivika — Caused by natural forces
cured by transcendence via spiritual practices

Annapurna Sarada is the president of SRV Associations and an assistant teacher for the sangha. She also writes on spiritual topics at Medium.com.

Wisdom Facets From the Gem of Truth

Sri Ramakrishna

"You Must know One Thing; I am Awakened"

"Some beings call Buddha an atheist. He was not an atheist. He simply could not express his inner experiences in words. Do you know what 'Buddha' means? It is to become one with Bodha, Pure Intelligence, by meditating upon That which is of the nature of Pure Intelligence; it is to become Pure Intelligence Itself. And he realized svarupa, the true nature of the Self. Then one attains a state that is something between asti, *is*, and nasti, *is not*. You see, asti and nasti are both attributes of Prakriti. The Reality is beyond both."

(Gospel of Sri Ramakrishna)

God or Mammon: Make your Choice

"When the mind is united with God, one sees Him very near, in one's own heart. But you must remember one thing. The more you realize this unity, the further your mind is withdrawn from worldly things." *(Gospel of Sri Ramakrishna)*

Thinking Ahead

"No doubt a good man must experience some of his karma, a little of its effect, but the bulk of his karma is cancelled by the Lord's Name. A man was born blind of one eye. This was his punishment for a certain misdeed he had committed in his past birth, and the punishment was to remain with him for six more births. He, however, took a bath in the Ganges, which gives one liberation. This meritorious action could not cure his blindness, but it saved him from future births."

(Gospel of Sri Ramakrishna)

After the Passing

"Before I go I will make the entire thing public. When people in large numbers come to know about the greatness of this body, then Mother will take it back. The devotees will be sifted into inner and outer circles in the end. Thereafter, a band of my young disciples, with Narendra as their leader, will in due course renounce the world and devote themselves to the realization of God and service of the humanity."

(Gospel of Sri Ramakrishna)

Holy Mother, Sri Sarada Devi

The Most Important Thing

"All that you have to do is to pay obeisance to God at the end of the day. If one firmly takes ahold of a single, noble idea, one does not have to perform any other discipline. Our Master, Sri Ramakrishna, has said so many powerful things throughout His life, and they were all true. All that one has to do, then, is to select one of these great statements and concentrate upon it." *(Sri Sarada Vijnanagita)*

Mother of the Incarnations

"After the passing away of the Master I have been living in the world and ministering to the spiritual needs of the people. The spiritual consorts of other incarnations did not do such a thing. In those cases it was the followers of the incarnations that took care of spiritual ministrations. But our Master saw the Divine Mother in all beings. This time He has left me behind in order to teach the Motherhood of God to the world." *(The Compassionate Mother)*

A Few True Friends

"There are many devotees who could help me. They could even give me ten-thousand rupees. But how many are there that could feel that this is 'my' Mother's burden? After all, how many are there who are truly our own? Just a few! The Master used to remark, 'How many, indeed, belong to the inner circle?'" *(The Compassionate Mother)*

Color Me Inward

"I have granted mental, or inward sannyasa, to a few householders. These are the 'hidden yogis,' as the Master used to say — inwardly ochre clad, outwardly like ordinary human beings — like Narada. For, the outward garb of a monk often nourishes his ego, and thus becomes the cause of bondage for many." *(The Compassionate Mother)*

Wisdom Facets From the Gem of Truth

Painting by Swami Tadatmananda

Swami Vivekananda

Oh, Snapper of This World's Chains
"India is the only place where, with all its faults, the soul finds its freedom, its God. All this Western pomp is only vanity, only bondage of the soul. Never in my life have I realized more forcibly the vanity of this world. May the Lord break the bondage of all — may all come out of maya — is the constant prayer of Vivekananda." *(Swami Vivekananda Vijnanagita)*

Iron Chain, Gold Chain, & God's Chain
"Without the unbroken chain of discipleship nothing really spiritual can be done. Is it mere child's play? To have no connection whatsoever and still to call oneself a disciple, is idiocy. So if a man refuses to go on in the right way, turn him out. Nothing, I say, can be done without the chain of discipleship." *(Swami Vivekananda Vijnanagita)*

So Blast Your Karma!
"What brings us here? Our past deeds. What takes us out? Our own deeds here. So on and on we go. We have thrown the network of our own actions around ourselves. We have set the law of causation in motion and find it hard to get ourselves out of it. We have set the wheel in motion and are being crushed under it. And so the philosophy of Karma Yoga teaches us that we are uniformly being bound by our own actions, good and bad."
(Swami Vivekananda in Jnana Yoga)

Sri Ramakrishna Guru Deva Samprite
"Any of you can join any party you like; I have no objection, no, not in the least. But traveling this world over, I find that save and except His circle alone, everywhere else thought and act are at variance. In those who belong to Him I have the utmost love, the utmost confidence. Call me one-sided if you will, but there you have my bona fide avowal. If but a thorn pricks the foot of one who has surrendered to Sri Ramakrishna, it makes my bones ache; all others I love."
(Swami Vivekananda Vijnanagita)

Disciples & Devotees of Sri Ramakrishna

Who is the Real Stranger here?
"With the advent of Sri Ramakrishna a new age has dawned. Let all find the way of peace. Whoever walks His path will be immersed in bliss. We must make all the people of this earth our very own. Let none be a stranger or an outsider. If there must be an outsider it should be this ego — I, me, and mine." *(Swami Premananda, Memories of a Loving Soul)*

To Truly Honor a Savior....
"We do not honor a Savior merely by belonging to a creed founded in His name, or by offering Him lip praise. Only as we learn to shape ourselves after the model of His own do we prove ourselves worthy of Him. And this can be done only by living His teachings. Otherwise, as Lord Jesus said, 'And why call ye me, 'Lord, Lord,' and do not the things which I say?.'" *(Swami Paramananda, Christ and the Oriental Ideal)*

Who Shall I Talk with Today?
"I was very much blessed to attend a Western style Christmas party given by Sister Devamata at her house for members of the Math and close-in devotees. After the service there was reading from the Bible, and prasadam was distributed. As the sister was reading from the Bible, Christ suddenly stood before the altar dressed in a long, blue cloak. He talked to me for some time. It was a blessed moment."
(Swami Brahmananda, in Sri Ramakrishnananda, Apostle to the South)

Do Not Intensify an Impure Mind
"Even the jivanmuktas live after attaining knowledge. It is a matter of realization alone. Mere questions do not help much. Be pure. Give up evil thoughts and work hard. Gradually you will come to understand everything. It is impossible to understand these things without intuitive knowledge. Practice hard, but don't take up spiritual practice in the spirit of forced labor."

(Swami Saradananda, Glimpses of a Great Soul)

SCRIPTURAL SAYINGS
of the World's Religious Traditions

"The sincere and qualified disciple should think that all things in this world are subject to a constant transformation – that all things in the past are a dream, that all things in the present are like a flash of lightning, and all things of the future are like images that arrive spontaneously into existence."

"It is thus, by the hands of the illumined ones, that this study of principles called Sankhya Yoga is produced, a spiritual science which consists of saying adamantly, 'I am not that; this is not mine; this is not my Self.' It is a science definitive, intrinsically pure, and free from all kinds of doubt, a science absolute and unique – the original wisdom of divine nature and origin which always and unerringly returns one to the Source."

"I have strayed like a lost sheep seeking outside me that which was within. I have run about the streets and places of the world, this great city, seeking Thee and I have not found Thee because I sought Thee ill and came not to the place where Thou wert. Thou wert within me and I sought Thee without. Thou wert near and I sought Thee at a distance. If I had gone where Thou wert, I certainly would have met Thee."

"Is it such a fast that I have chosen, a day for a man to afflict his soul? Is it to bow down his head as a bulrush and spread sackcloth and ashes under him? Wilt thou call this a fast and an acceptable day to the Lord? Rather, is this not the day I have chosen, in which to loose the bonds of wickedness, to undo heavy burdens, to let the oppressed go free, to deal thy bread to the hungry, to bring in the poor that were cast out of my house, and when you seest the naked, cover them up – all so that you will not hide thyself from thine own kind? Then shall the real fast begin, and light break forth as the morning sun."

"If thou remainest in isolation, thou shalt never be able to travel the path of the Spirit; a guide is needed. Go not alone by thyself, enter not as a blind man into that ocean. Since thou art utterly ignorant ask what thou shouldst do to issue out of the pit of this world, and fail not to apprehend a sure guide."

"That wise one who recognizes spiritual instruction, and duly acts upon it, will certainly arrive at supreme mastery. That one loves to ask in order to extend his knowledge to the fullest. But the foolish one who considers only his own opinion only ends up becoming narrower than he was."

ON THE HAJ

Lex Hixon's Transforming Pilgrimage to Mecca

Ardent spiritual practitioner and adept participant in several of the religious traditions of the world, and the original founder of our SRV Associations, Lex Hixon became a Sheikh of the Jerrahi Sufi movement of Istanbul later in life. This *In The Spirit* radio program was recorded live on November 9th, 1980, shortly after his return from pilgrimage to Mecca.

Good afternoon. This is WBAI radio, the program, *In The Spirit*. This is Lex Hixon, and I am happy to be back with you. I have just returned home from Saudi Arabia for a few weeks. And some of you may remember that before I left, I read a chapter from Malcom X's autobiography on the Haj, or the pilgrimage to Mecca, on the program.

The autobiography of Malcolm X is one of the classics of American literature. However, too few people concentrate on that chapter on The Haj. They don't realize what a transformation that the great Malcolm X went through when he went to Mecca on the pilgrimage. And I can't claim to be anywhere in the same league as Malcolm X as an observer of American society, and as someone who has paid their dues. But somehow through the Grace of Allah, I was able to make that pilgrimage, make that Haj, and I saw some of the things that Malcolm X saw, as far as the revolutionary way that people from the first world, second world, third world, fourth world, or any other socio-political world that might emerge, can join and merge and be brothers and sisters in Islam. That was one of the things I saw. I saw other things too, on other levels of being.

And I was inviting a guest this morning to do this first show, who is a British scholar of Islam and a British muslim who came with me on pilgrimage, and oddly enough he called me up at the very last minute and said that he just could not make it. And I had to laugh, because I was really going to hide behind him and interview him about the pilgrimage in order to not to have to reveal my own feelings and own experiences. And I think I was doing that from a good motivation, which is really that I do not feel that I am mature enough to say something about the Haj. I don't think that my practice and association with Islam is deep enough, and it has not gone on long enough.

So I find myself standing before you in a kind of nakedness that WBAI does aspire to create over the air. I suppose that it makes good radio, and for truthful and revealing radio. So I do not have anyone to interview, and no one to hide behind, so whether I like it or not I had better share with you the experiences I had in Saudi Arabia — the humorous ones, the serious ones — and with some idea that not all of you are necessarily interested in Islam. Although, the idea of the pilgrimage or the Haj has become an almost mythical and romantic story in European and Western cultures. So, I doubt whether there is not anyone who is faintly interested in what it was like to be in Mecca.

In the light of this overall disinterest in Islam, one might ask what's the justification of spending an hour in the middle of the day talking about this? And it is just simply this, which is also a principle behind this free radio station, that if someone goes deeply into a specific experience that might be relevant to only a few people, if the person does it honestly and intelligently, and with a little bit of humor, somehow this can become a revelatory experience for everyone. It also casts light on many issues.

And so I am going to be doing a series of programs on Islam for the next week or so, and I don't want you to think that another special interest group has come to WBAI, and now the station is going to be Radio Islam in New York or something like that. It is more that somehow I feel that there is a very profound and vibrant message in Islam for the whole world, and more precisely for our country and its many different sub-cultures. It is not a theological message. You could almost say that it is a very practical and sociological message, but a social message that has spiritual roots.

Malcolm X, when he first arrived in Jedda at the airport there, had to spend a day or so securing his passport, which just about everyone has to do. The Turkish Dervishes and Islamic sisters and brothers who I went with, we had to spend about 24 hours in the airport. Because when you have over 100,000 people arriving by plane each day, it is kind of hard to process the passports and the baggage and all that. About two to three million people come to the Haj, and came this year to the Haj, which occurs in the space of a week or so, and during this time of year. It is a holy month, especially for Haj.

And Malcolm X said, in his autobiography, that he did not think that a movie camera had ever shot a scene like that, with so many diverse races, colors, and hues that he saw in the airport in Jedda. And I would agree. While we were going through the 24 hours of waiting, I stood for hours just captivated by the many people who had come. You see people who were obviously from Russia, Bulgaria, and Yugoslavia, with their high boots on, dressed in very thick clothes that could not possibly be used in warm weather. I saw many people from Africa. There was a whole group of Chinese Muslims from Hong Kong, staying near us in that airport shelter, a several story building that houses about fifty people in each of its rooms. They all looked like Taoist sages, each with little beards, except they were Islamic, and they were doing their prayers.

At that time, in the airport, many of the pilgrims had not yet donned their pilgrim's garb, which are just white. For the men, two plain sheets of cloth, and for the women, white dresses. And by the way, the women are not allowed to veil their faces while on pilgrimage. So with no veils, one had a beautiful chance to observe the Islamic women. When you look into their eyes they do not look away. So it is not like their personalities have been effaced by Islam, as some think; they look directly at you. There is a tremendous strength and honesty in them.

go back to your country or nation, or your family, or wherever you left, you come back with a tremendous sense of being born fresh, and of being a great deal more careful, and dedicated to one's human life and towards all that lives. Well, knowing human nature, I can say that this type of thing can fade, but I can

> "....you are engaging in a once in a lifetime act that is a culmination of your lifetime. People who do make the Haj, they get called Hajis. In some countries they adopt that word into their names. It was such a transformation for them, it became a new way of looking at their entire life."

So, in the airport, there were some people in religious garb, but most of them were in their national dress. There were many, many Nigerians, since Africa has a large Muslim population.

So, as Malcolm X tells it, he was in the airport for about seven hours before, as he put it, his entire understanding of race relations dissolved, and got turned around. I did not have that particular background that he had, where that had been as burning an issue for me, but the burning issue for me has been the diversity of religions in the world, and the separation between them. So what was confirmed for me was the unity of mankind, or of humankind. Also, the unity between men and women. I went there with a certain amount of consciousness around feminist issues, and I saw a fundamental equality happening there. So, it was, initially, for me, a great experience of the unity of humankind. Where else can you be with two or three million people from almost every country in the world?

Our group was one of the very few American ones that we saw. But I did meet one man from Texas. He was a kind of gnarled looking older man. He looked like he would be wearing a ten-gallon hat, usually, and he said that when he was in Morocco, thirty years earlier, he had embraced Islam, and had been living a quiet life as a Muslim somewhere in Texas. Then he came on the Haj. It is a once in a lifetime requirement in Islam that one do this pilgrimage, so I saw many older people there who may have decided that they are about ready to fade out of this world, and they want to make the culmination of their life.

And I saw a tremendous amount of younger people too, with an atmosphere that runs from a kind of gaiety of being on a picnic or a festival, to a really, really, profound sense of seriousness that knows that you are engaging in a once in a lifetime act that is a culmination of your lifetime. People who do make the Haj, they get called Hajis. In some countries they adopt that word into their names. It was such a transformation for them, it became a new way of looking at their entire life.

So it is not only people such as Malcolm X and myself who come from non-Islamic cultures who get transformed by the Haj, it is Muslims themselves as well. And it is essentially an experience of death, because the pilgrims garb is that of a shroud. And in fact, many people save their pilgrim's garb to wrap themselves up with in burial. It, the Haj, really is a kind of death, then, and when you come out the other side, it is a rebirth. And when you

still feel it strongly in myself, and I have a feeling that for most Hajis it is something that stays with them for a lifetime — even if it is not always palpably there, but is somewhere in their psyche. And it can be called upon.

I have no idea how to talk about this from here. I had not planned to do it this way, and even feel regrets about having to talk about it. But it is so recent for me, and there is a special intimacy around radio, that I feel that I should speak to all of you as friends. That way you will get the most out of this experience. I am not a reporter from the BBC telling you about something; I am just revealing it to you personally, with a certain amount of trust that you will find something relevant in it for yourself.

From Jedda, in Saudi Arabia, from the airport, we finally made it to Medina. Medina is the great holy place established by Mohammed, may the peace and blessings of Allah be upon him. As the prophet himself said, *"Abraham established the Kaaba in Mecca and made it a holy place."* This is in the Islamic tradition. Mohammed said, *"As Abraham made Mecca a holy city, I make Medina."*

Arriving about the time of sunset in Medina, after not really having seen anything of the Arabian countryside, just being inside the airport in Jedda, which is a modern and fairly Western style airport — except for the fact that there are hundreds and thousands of people sleeping all over — it was the first glimpse of the countryside of Arabia, and it really is a bit of a shock. The impact and power of it is very great, and as Malcolm X said, these mountains look like some kind of slag heap. It is really not a very kind description, but they do look like they are molten and suddenly just frozen in that position. The eye thinks that it is seeing trees on the tops, but those are really just rock formations. And the desert itself seems to be just crumbled rock. It is a very, very tough landscape, but a powerful one, and a numinous one.

So we spent four days in Medina, which is part of the pilgrimage itself; often people go there after they go to Mecca. And you are supposed to do eight days of prayer in Medina, as it is the city of prayer. As you know, the Muslim prayer is five times a day. So you have to do forty sessions of prayer. We were only there for four days, but we made up the extra prayers. And the huge Mosque in Medina, called the Prophet's Mosque, contains the tomb of the Prophet and of his family, and some of the early Califs. It is an extremely potent place spiritually, and emotionally, and in every other way.

The mosque itself is huge; it must be about four city blocks, and with a big open courtyard in the middle. And there were so many of the faithful there that — imagine the morning prayer there at 5 am — if you got there at, say, four am, you might find a place to lay your prayer cloth and just barely be able to see the mosque in the distance, there were so many people. And evidently later, when people come from Mecca, it is unbelievably dense.

But I can remember sitting in the hotel room, and during noon prayer the sun was so unbelievably hot that I did not go out to the mosque for prayer, but just did them in the hotel room. I can remember laying out the prayer rug on the hotel room floor and looking out the window just about the time when the call to bulate the tomb. And one of the fascinating things that the women will be particularly interested in is that there was as much devotion shown at the tomb of Fatima, the Prophet's daughter. And the Prophet did say, in a mystical sense, "She is a part of me." The divine feminine aspect is represented there very intensely.

When we arrived in Medina, that night, I had a dream which I think I should share with you, because this is where the depth of the experience comes in. You know, you can make many social and even philosophical associations when you go on a trip and such, but when you dream something its an experience that is happening very deep in your psyche. It is not happening on the surface, nor is it observable from the surface. And par-

Millions coming and going on Haj in Mecca, 2016

prayer was happening. And all that I can see over the entire city were pilgrims in lines, all getting ready for the prayer. And there were so many speakers in the city that even in the hotel room, with the air conditioning going on, I could still clearly hear the chanting of the Koran and the entire prayer, and I could join with it, and bow at the proper time, and kneel at the proper time. And when the time came to chant "Amin," or "Amen," you could just hear that word coming up from the entire city.

And during the middle of the night — we slept very little at night and usually caught some sleep in the day and stayed up all night because it was cooler and less crowded then — we could go into the Prophet's Mosque and go around the tomb, circumam-
ticularly within the Islamic tradition of which I am a part, with the Jerrahi Dervishes from Istanbul, all the teaching comes through dream. And when you have the dream, you take the dream to the Sheikh and tell the dream, and there is a spontaneous interchange when a Sheikh gives the interpretation. And that alchemical combination between your dream and the Sheikh's interpretation, what happens when those two things are brought together, actually causes you to step up a spiritual level. That's the method by which this particular Dervish Order works, and many of the mystical orders in Islam.

So I was traveling with my Sheikh, and it was a great honor and blessing to be with a man who has been on the Haj twelve or thirteen times himself, and who speaks Arabic, and who has a profound and mystical connection with everything that is going on. So I was able to experience the depth of certain things, rather than just the surface of the rituals of the pilgrimage — which are very powerful in themselves, but which are not a deep part of my particular soul because I have never been that connected with conventional religion, although I have a great respect for it. I have always been looking for the depth that is behind the religion and the scriptures.

That night, arriving in Medina in the prophet's holy city I did have a dream. I got to sleep about two in the morning, and had just washed my hair, and I had a dream in about the space of an hour. When I woke up again, and it must have been about an hour, my hair was still wet. And the dream was this:

I was going to be allowed to ask the Prophet — may the peace and blessings of Allah be upon him — about the highest mystical teaching of Islam. So I formulated the question. I didn't see the prophet, but I knew that the question was being conveyed to him. And the question was this:

"In the Koran, we read that all the thoughts and actions of all beings are praising Allah, whether they are good or bad.
Is everything that is happening in the Universe just a form of praising the ultimate Source of the universe?"

And the minute I asked the question I woke up instantly. And

A couple of days later I had the chance to tell this experience to the Sheikh to get his interpretation, all through a very lovely Arabic woman who was with us and who could speak very fluent English. She served as a wonderful translator. And when she told the experience to Sheikh Muzaffer, he smiled and said, "You are very fortunate, it is an excellent dream. It means that your Haj has been accepted." These words came to me with an unbelievable naturalness, but authoritativeness, like just right out of the blue. I just didn't even hold the concept that the pilgrimage was something to be accepted; I assumed it was just sort of automatic. I hadn't opened up to the idea that, of course, its a matter of how deep your pilgrimage is as to whether it is accepted as a full pilgrimage by Allah. The impact of what he told me not only caused tears to come to my eyes, but I noticed, too, that the translator was weeping at having heard this.

So I will not easily forget that I went to Medina and Mecca, which was in the Islamic year of 1400, 1400 years after the Prophet arrived in Medina from Mecca. He stayed in Mecca for something like 13 years as a Prophet, trying to have his message heard. Mecca was the center for holy pilgrimage at that time for the pre-Islamic period, and the people were very stubborn, not wanting to hear the fresh interpretation, the fresh revelation. And so finally, after bitter persecution and suffering, he went to Medina, and he lived only ten years there before his death, and

> "This sura of the Koran tells of the oneness and completeness of the Ultimate Reality, which in Arabic is called Allah, and affirms that this Ultimate Reality really does not bring to birth anything that is separate from Itself, nor bring into being anything that is more primary than Itself. In other words, It is just a oneness and completeness which Is. And so naturally everything that is, is the praise of this Ultimate Reality, and everything is the expression of it"

it was a strange kind of waking up, because I am a very sound sleeper and a reluctant waker, but I was so instantly awake that it was like being in a quite different state of consciousness. And, there was no question, for instance, of lying down and going back to sleep, which is very unusual for me. And in that state of clearness and awareness, the answer to the question came, and it came in the form of a short sura from the Koran, the Koran often spoken of as being the Prophet's miracle.

This sura of the Koran tells of the oneness and completeness of the Ultimate Reality, which in Arabic is called Allah, and affirms that this Ultimate Reality really doesn't bring to birth anything that is separate from Itself, nor bring into being anything that is more primary than Itself. In other words, It is just a oneness and completeness which Is. And so naturally everything that is, is the praise of this Ultimate Reality, and everything is the expression of it.

Well, actually this answer didn't hit in any philosophical way, it hit me like a beam of intense energy. So I went into the bathroom to take ablutions before offering some prayer, and tears were just streaming out of my eyes due to the intensity of this particular answer.

in that ten years all of Arabia embraced Islam. So it was a very fruitful and powerful ten years. And some of that power you feel in Medina, the city of prayer, where the Prophet's tomb is, and where there is such sweetness and richness of spiritual atmosphere.

From there we went to Mecca, and upon entering Mecca and walking its streets one begins to be stripped bare. The power, the millions of people on the streets, the whole atmosphere there, is almost terrifying. It certainly was terrifying to me, and I thought at first it was just a cultural thing, but then I realized that it was on the spiritual level too. There is this raw, transcendent energy which completely strips you away from anything that you are holding onto. And of course, by this time you are dressed in your pilgrim's garb which is your shroud, and you are beginning to experience that the pilgrimage to the Kaaba is a form of death — a form of death to the mundane world, death to the selfish, personal world.

There are many steps that one goes through in Mecca on the pilgrimage, one of which is going to camp in the valley in Mina, which is many miles outside of Mecca, a kind of vast, barren valley, which at that time, of course, is filled with millions of tents.

A couple of million people have to go up there and camp. The logistics are just impossible to imagine, but we somehow found our tent and spent the night there.

The next day one goes to Mount Arafat, which is many miles distant, and some of the pilgrims walk all these distances. A lot of them ride buses, and vehicles of every description. And you don't just have one road going between Mina and Arafat, they have something like ten roads, and still the traffic jams are beyond belief. I mean, when I got back to New York City I thought it was just a quiet, little town. First of all, the space is totally unutilized in New York. The sidewalks are empty. No one is sitting around; no one is sleeping; no one is cooking tea. As far as the sound levels, few in New York blow their horn. An angry cab driver, maybe an occasional truck driver does, but in Mecca people drive with their horns on, and occasionally they turn them off, like when they stop. But the moment they put their foot on the accelerator, they put their thumbs on the horn.

So, New York seems like a really quiet place. Also, people think of New York as a real high energy place. I have to say, and I am just giving you my honest experience, compared to Mecca during pilgrimage, New York's energy is very moderate. There was such high energy there it was just like being tumbled along in an intense river in spate, a springtime river. And it was essentially on the level of the psyche, although we did go through many problems and inconveniences on the physical level, though not nearly as bad as some of the pilgrims. No matter how well you planned for Mecca, how well you were prepared, you cannot be sure that things will happen the way you think they should.

For instance when we went to Mount Arafat, which is one of the most powerful days of the pilgrimage where you spend the entire day on this craggy, rocky mountainside, and in 115 degree weather — you can have a tent over you, but we could not find our tent, so we ended up sitting on the roadside with the simplest of pilgrims who had absolutely nothing.

We sat there the entire day, and Sheikh Muzaffer was sitting on a thin, grass mat placed there on the hot concrete, just sitting there all day with buses driving by and exhaust fumes everywhere, and people going to the bathroom along the side of the road, and just total chaos. And he was joyous. Because, as I found out later, and particularly when you go to Mount Arafat, that is the ultimate point when everything is supposed to be stripped away from you, and you are left only with Allah, with the Light of Allah. Someone asked the Sheikh how he was, and he said, "Ah, the Light! There is such a beautiful Light on Mount Arafat!"

Towards the end of the day at sunset, which is a very powerful time, a couple of trucks and buses that were next to us wanted to pull out, so we had to take down the shelter that we made. They pulled out with a great deal of yelling, and exhaust, and they drove right in front of the Sheikh about five feet away, and he was still sitting there, oblivious, doing his prayer. And it was a very powerful prayer that contained the One-thousand-and-One Names of Allah. It was the prayer that had been revealed by the angel, Gabriel, to the blessed Prophet, saying to the Prophet that in his battles he no longer needed to wear armor. This is taken in the Muslim tradition in a very mystical sense, that if you chant this prayer, and can absorb it, you reach a level where you do not have to be armored in the psychological sense; you can be completely naked and still be protected.

Then, of course, there was the circumambulation of the Kaaba, which we did on two separate times, doing twenty-one circuits in all. Also, as a part of the ceremony, one runs between two small hills near the Kaaba. The wife of Abraham, Hagar, tradition says that she ran between those two hills looking for water. Many of these things are totally indescribable, and I am just giving you a shorthand of what went on. Some of you have probably seen pictures of Mecca in National Geographic. All I can say is, look at that picture and try to imagine what it is like.

The deep spiritual thing that I realized later is that I didn't have any deep spiritual experiences on Mount Arafat or at the Kaaba; it was all a stripping away. There was no light and delight. There were no grand insights. Sometimes I wondered why I was even there. Everything was stripped away, even the sense of connection with Islam was stripped away. It wasn't until all that was over that I had a second dream that I want to share with you, which clarified spiritually for me what was going on. And this was after we got back from our last circuits of the Kaaba.

I went to sleep after the morning prayer, after staying up all night, and went to sleep feeling totally empty, yet with a certain feeling of joy that it was over, but not with a sense of any spiritual significance around it all. And I had a dream that for what seemed like a couple of hours I was just repeating over and over again, "Ya Salam." Salam is one of the mystical 99 Names of Allah, which means, "O Thou perfectly Peaceful One." And occasionally I would wake up for a time, seeing my brothers around me sleeping, and I felt like this Peace was coming down not just on me, but upon them as well, and upon everything. Then I would fall asleep again and repeat, "Ya Salam, Ya Salam."

When I woke up, later that morning, I really was transformed; I had really had some sort of rebirth. Even physically I felt totally refreshed. And I went to the Shiekh and told him this dream, and he said, "Yes, that only confirms the fact that your Haj has been accepted, has been acceptable in the sight of Allah." And he also said that "Allah is sending you His Salams."

Lex Hixon (Nur al-Jerrahi) received his Ph.D. in World Religions from Columbia University in 1976. He then became an adept practitioner of several of the world's sacred traditions. From 1971 to 1984 he conducted a weekly radio show in New York City called "In The Spirit," interviewing spiritual teachers from around the world. An enlightened spiritual teacher, he guided many souls along their chosen path. Among his books are *Great Swan, Mother of the Universe, Heart of the Koran, Atom from the Sun of Knowledge, Mother of the Buddhas,* and *Living Buddha Zen.* For more information inquire at: www.lexhixon.org

◆ *Jamgon Kongtrul Rinpoche*

TIBETAN BUDDHA DHARMA

The Wide Open Blue Sky of Enlightened Mind

So, starting in a rather traditional mode, we have started out the program chanting a sacred Tibetan text and scripture. Now we want to talk to Jamgong Kongtrul Rinpoche himself, here on *In The Spirit* on WBAI Radio.

When I first saw Jamgong Kontrul Rinpoche it was on Maui in the mountains, on a very windy day in which the clouds were literally being swept from the skies. He was acting at that time as translator for the Karmapa. He was also giving out teachings on Buddha Dharma. Then a questioner asked him that since Karmapa was not his guru, should he visualize his own guru, or the Karmapa in his meditations. Jamgong Kontrul Rinpoche pointed to the sky and said, *"The blue sky is not the property of any nation lying under it. In the same way Buddha Dharma does not belong only to one guru."*

I want to ask the Rinpoche if he could comment on that point some more, through his translator who is here with him in the studio. [translator communicates the question]

Rinpoche: In the process of initiation by a guru, the spiritual energy of body, speech, and mind of the teacher is transmitted to the body, speech and mind of the disciple, and Rinpoche's response that day on Maui was that, just as we are dealing with the space, or sky, we regard it in terms of specific geographical locations. Just as the sky in New York is not different than the sky over other countries, we regard awareness as transcendent in the same way. There is a continuum in space that transcends the discontinuity of geography, and in the same way mind and consciousness, and particularly enlightened mind, has a continuum beyond individuals who embody that enlightened mind.

Beside that, we should recognize that one who is enlightened, in the way His Holinesss the Karmapa is, is endowed with a compassion that expresses that enlightenment which transcends the distinctions between various people, and expresses a complete unity. Through that, His Holiness, on some levels, can be seen as the teacher of all living things. And so from that point of view, as well, there is no need for these concerns about the distinctions between enlightened gurus.

Lex Hixon: In the song that the Karmapa wrote in his third manifestation as Ranjon Dorje, he writes about this blue sky of mind, and I quote: *"All dharmas are phantoms of the mind, and mind is no mind; the mind's nature is empty. Though empty, everything unceasingly arises from it."* Could Rinpoche possibly comment on this? [translator communicates question]

Rinpoche: In the first line, where it states that all things that arise can be considered as nonexistent, it means that all that we know, we know in mind. We can't separate, in particular or in general, any aspect of Reality from the fact of mind, so that if we say that something is good, or that something is bad, or we determine that something is ugly, all of this judgement and all of this process of determining how they aren't or how they are, or might be, is a process that occurs in mind, and in perception, unless all that arises cannot be regarded separately from mind.

And then, where it says that mind is "no mind," "mind is emptiness," so that in terms of dealing with all the phenomena that exists, it seems that mind is something real. We go through this process of determining that everything that we experience occurs in mind, and so that seems to point to the fact that mind is something real. However, when we try to sit and ask, "What is mind," and work that out apart from all of the events and perceptions that occur in mind, we are left with nothing. We find that there is nothing that we can see, no concrete substance that we can seize, that allows us to say "this is mind." So we come to the conclusion, then, that there is no mind; mind is empty.

Rinpoche says that it is important here to remember that Buddhism at this juncture does not step into a merely nihilistic position to say that since mind is empty, that does not mean that there is nothing but an empty void, like some blank. Its not that at all, because in spite of the fact that there is nothing that can be conclusively determined, we still face this unceasing flow of events, thoughts, perceptions, feelings, ideas, conceptions that are all occurring in mind, all are occurring in consciousness. So we are faced with a paradox of sorts in which there is this unending play of mental events, but at the same time there is nothing that can be determined that can conclusively be called "mind."

[Rinpoche speaks, and translation]

And so, the direction that this points us to is that we can only discover the real nature of mind as the ground and foundation for all experience and all existence when we have left behind all of these simplistic judgments about existence and nonexistence, and reality and nonreality. So, pointing towards the goal of the study of the nature of mind in Buddhism, one then aspires to cut off all of these misguided judgments about reality, fixed ideas about being and nonbeing in order to really see the nature of mind, and of reality

[Rinpoche speaks, and more translation]

We should remember here that although these things are very easy to say, and very easy to speak of, that is very hard to fully realize the implications of these things. It is rather like watching a high diver going over a cliff into the water, and as he jumps from the cliff it looks like the easiest thing in the world, but when we get close to the edge we find our knees shaking a bit. We are all of a sudden extremely reticent to make the leap.

Lex Hixon: I want to ask Rinpoche, is it alright to discuss these matters even though we are unable to make the dive?

[translation of question, Rinpoche speaks, and translation]

Rinpoche: Here we are mostly taking about the Goal, the thing that is to be attained through this path and this practice. To know a bit about that may be helpful, particularly if we have a bit of aspiration, to either now or in the future, set out to achieve the vision that is pointed to in a work such as this. It can give us a bit of fortitude, a bit of encouragement in starting out. As far as the actual means by which this is realized, there are special sets of precepts which are to be worked out in experience in work for the teacher, and that material would not be appropriate for discussion of this sort.

Lex Hixon: Let me ask Rinpoche, and with just a rough understanding of what he said, that everything is the sky, and the sky goes on forever, and the earth, and objects, and people are like clouds in the sky, that somehow are born right out of the sky itself. Can you ask him if that is correct?

[translation of question, Rinpoche speaks, and translation]

Rinpoche: In your analogy, if the clouds are like the things that we deal with in the world, then what is space in the analogy?

Lex Hixon: The blue sky would be the mind, but there is another thing I want to ask him. It says in the text here, "Since there is no support for affirming or denying, may I understand the fallacy of alaya"....in other words, the fallacy that there is an underlying mind, even. So in my analogy, the blue sky would be the mind, and space, which is colorless, would be the Truth.

Translator: May I just point out here, that the verse is somewhat mistranslated. [laughter]

Lex Hixon: Okay, then leaving this verse out due to its translation, can you convey to Rinpoche my question, that is, if the blue sky is the mind, is there something that is beyond mind, for after all, when the sun sets the sky is not blue anymore.

[translation of question, Rinpoche speaks, and translation]

Rinpoche: We are getting to the problem of carrying analogies too far, because while as an immediate example of our experience we can refer to all the things that arise in the world as relating to mind as the constant play of clouds seems to relate to the sky, when we sit down and analyse it precisely we realize that beyond the sky clouds require wind and water in order to form, so the analogy breaks down when you try to press it too far. So we should just try to see the immediacy of the analogy rather than to try and make it a set model for explaining reality.

Lex Hixon: Then let me ask the question differently. Is there a difference between relative mind and absolute mind?

[translation of question, Rinpoche speaks, and translation]

Rinpoche: First, the actual nature of mind transcends the distinction between relative and absolute. But conventionally, in order to have a language to discuss it in the first place, we can refer to the abiding nature of mind as the Absolute.

Lex Hixon: So, when a teacher says that there is no real distinction between relative and absolute mind, or in this text, that the ordinary mind is the way, then they are just refusing to be conventional at that point.

[translation of question, Rinpoche speaks, and translation]

Rinpoche: The transcendence of the distinction between the relative and the absolute shouldn't be something that we take to another extreme, because ultimately that is transcended. While we are dealing with these conventional dualities, we are just beyond that distinction. Conventionally speaking, the realization of the real nature of the mind is the absolute, and the perception of just what appears to us on whatever level that we see it is what's relative. As long as we are working in our own lives and minds with dualistic thoughts and perceptions — and that is the real distinction that we have to deal with — so it doesn't suffice to say that the relative is just the same as the absolute.

Lex Hixon: The reason I asked that question was not just for an abstract philosophical reason, but it relates very strongly to the practical meditation practice. Because the text says, *"Knowing how to rest in the spontaneous, uncontrived flow,"* and in another place it states *"being free from mind constructions, it is the Mahamudra."* So, if Rinpoche will accept the analogy of clouds being dualistic thoughts and perceptions...when one is meditating in the Mahamudra style of meditation, do the clouds disappear, or does one float among them as they blow back and forth across the sky?

[translation of question, Rinpoche speaks, and translation]

Rinpoche: At this juncture we probably have to get back to the basic issue that we are addressing, and not so much the various analogies, and the ground to that station is the distinction between projections of mind, and mind free from all projections. So, when you are referring to the clouds those are just projections and various processes of projections in mind, and the sky itself being mind free from projections.

The definition of projection, in the sense that we are dealing with it here, is that in reference to what occurs in reality, we make judgments, we react, we have aversions and inclinations and attachments and so forth, that color our view of reality. These are all projections. Complete absence of these, and just dealing with reality as it is, without our creating any structures that impede the nature of reality, is mind free from projections.

In the teaching of meditation in the Kagyu school, because we are so involved with mental projections and structures in our mind based upon these projections, we start out with techniques that make use of these, and that put the aspect of mind into certain frameworks that allow for gradual refinement. Then ultimately, through that process, complete freedom from projection is eventually achieved; that is the goal of this path.

Lex Hixon: We certainly want to offer our profound thanks to Jamgong Kontrul Rinpoche and his translator for appearing here on "In The Spirit" and clarifying for us the Tibetan Buddhist teaching of the Kagyu lineage around the clear blue sky of Enlightened Mind.

Born in Lhasa, Tibet, Jamgon Kongtrul Rinpoche was recognized as an incarnation of the previous Jamgon Kongtrul by the late Sixteenth Gyalwa Karmapa, the supreme head of the Kagyu lineage. At the age of six, the young tulku left Tibet to join H.H. the Karmapa at Rumtek Monastery in Sikkim where he was raised by the Karmapa as one of his four "heart sons." Jamgon Kongtrul Rinpoche accompanied the Karmapa to the United States in 1976 and 1980 and in recent years carried out the Karmapa's work, inspiring and teaching large numbers of students in Asia as well as in Europe and the United States.

◆ *Swami Brahmeshananda*

THE SEARCH FOR EVERLASTING BLISS

Or: The Unrelenting Trap of Momentary Pleasures

We are pleased to be able to reprint Swami Brahmeshanandaji's article, "Search for Everlasting Bliss," first published as the April 1999 editorial of The Vedanta Kesari, a monthly cultural and spiritual magazine of the Ramakrishna Order.

There is a Buddhist saying: If you want happiness for an hour take a nap. If you want happiness for a day go on a shopping spree. If you want happiness for a month go on a honeymoon. If you want happiness for a year inherit a fortune. If you want happiness for a lifetime help someone else. If you want eternal happiness know yourself. To this, we may add, "If you want momentary happiness, indulge in sense enjoyments."

Joy, happiness, bliss, enjoyment, and pleasure are some of the words often used interchangeably to express a favorable feeling. Satisfaction, peace, and contentment are a few more words with more or less similar import. Their opposites are suffering, misery, sorrow, pain, dissatisfaction, discontent, and so on. Thus although we have used the word happiness, this word may not be exactly appropriate for what all human beings are aspiring for. This is because happiness has its opposite in misery, and the two always go together. To seek happiness without misery is futile, and can never happen. What one actually must strive for is a state beyond both happiness and misery, pleasure and pain — a state of undisturbed peace and tranquility, a state of bliss beyond the opposite pairs of joy and sorrow. This state is called *ananda* in Sanskrit. It is a quality and a characteristic of a pure and tranquil mind — a *sattvika* mind. The attainment of this state of unalloyed, superlative bliss — *niratishaya ànanda* — has been the search of humanity through eternity, and has often formed the central theme of the Hindu scriptures.

Bliss Through Sense Enjoyments

All human beings get happiness in some form or the other and aspire and struggle for more. But often they do not get unalloyed bliss. Happiness is often mixed with much unhappiness and misery. Sense-enjoyments, being associated with innumerable evils and problems, cannot be considered real happiness. They simply give momentary pleasure. According to Vedanta, even the momentary happiness we get in sense enjoyment is really a reflection of the bliss of the *Atman* on the tranquil, *sattvika* state of mind, attained, even though for a moment, due to the satisfaction of a desire for sense-objects. Thus, even this little sense enjoyment, if carefully scrutinized, can lead one to the everlasting bliss of *Brahman* — *Brahmananda*.

What does a man of knowledge, a *brahmajnani*, do when encountering sense objects? Does he not experience sense pleasures? All saints and sages, including Sri Ramakrishna and Swami Vivekananda, did enjoy sense pleasures like eating a delicious dish, listening to melodious songs, etc. But there is a world of difference between their enjoyments and ours. Even at the moment of sense enjoyment, their attention used to remain directed towards *Brahman*. A part of their mind always remained turned towards God, even at the time of sense enjoyment. This is the reason why they would very often get merged in *samadhi* soon after listening to a song. Secondly, they were never dependent on sense-objects for their bliss and happiness. By imitating them we too can escape from becoming dependent slaves of the senses. Let us not run after the sense-objects. We may enjoy them as they are presented before us in the natural course of events, without hankering for them, but let us be fully aware that the joy which we are getting is not from the objects themselves, but is due to the reflection of the bliss of the Self. This will protect us from becoming slaves of the senses.

Bliss Through Sleep and Tranquility

During the state of deep sleep one gets maximum bliss. But unfortunately our identity and our experience are both shrouded in ignorance in that state, since it is a state of *tamas*. Can we not experience the subject-object-free state of deep sleep while remaining awake? Yes. The scriptures say that this is possible and that everyone must try for it. According to Advaita Vedanta we experience the bliss of the unlimited *Brahman*, the One-without-a-second, in sleep, although it is covered with ignorance. In that state, the mental modification (*vritti*) of ignorance reflects the superlative bliss of the Pure *Atman*.

It is a common experience that, after sleep, one does not like to get up all of a sudden, but wishes to remain lying down in a silent half-awake state for some time. There is a state just prior to falling asleep, and a state immediately after sleep, when there are no mental modifications, nor is the mind covered with the veil of ignorance or sleep. It is believed that the bliss of *Brahman* is experienced then, and we must try to prolong this silent state as much as we can.

There could be moments, apart from those just before and after sleep, when the mind might become intensely quiet and yet alert. The mind may become quiet on listening to a sweet melody, or on seeing beautiful, natural scenery. Gazing at the tranquil ocean or the sky may quieten the mind. These states of quietness are technically called *tushnim sthiti* in Vedanta, and adepts recommend that one must not allow these precious moments to pass by unnoticed. One must recognize them and try to remain in them as long as possible. Even without external stimuli or inducers like music or a beautiful natural landscape, the mind may become quiet of its own, especially when, for some reason, the three gunas perfectly balance each other. These are the moments when the bliss of the *Atman* bursts forth. Such moments must be recognized and prolonged as much as possible.

According to Shankaracharya, every thought (*chitta vritti*) that arises in our mind has three components: the thought wave proper; the reflection of the light of Consciousness or the Self in it which makes it appear conscious; and the Pure Consciousness forming the substratum of the two. To explain this, the great *acharya* gives the example of a string of beads. The connecting string is single and present in all the beads, though the beads are many. The beads stand for the thought-waves and the reflections of consciousness on them, and the continuous string stands for the uninterrupted presence of pure consciousness in all the thought waves. But there is a small interval between one bead and the next where the string is visible. This represents the period between the subsidence of one thought wave and the origin of another thought wave, when pure consciousness is visible, as it were. Now, can we prolong the duration of the thoughtless period, the period between the subsiding of the first and the origin of the second thought-wave? Yes, this can be done by *Yoga*. By *Yoga* practice the thought waves can be quietened, and the duration between two successive *vrittis* can be prolonged.

While what has just been written might be theoretically true, and some spiritual aspirants might be able to extend the tranquil moment by persistent effort, there are two dangers. First, if we are physically and mentally dull and not sufficiently alert — as is generally the case before and after sleep — we may become all the more merged in dullness and inertia instead of bliss. Secondly, trying to keep the mind free from all thought waves in a tranquil state may lead to a state of void, which is not desirable. The attainment of a tranquil thoughtless state with awareness is possible only when we do all our daily activities with alertness and awareness. Because of these dangers it is advisable to fill a tranquil and quietened mind with the thought of the Divine with form and attributes or without form. It is always preferable in the initial stages to raise one thought wave to the exclusion of others, instead of making the mind altogether thoughtless.

Bliss Through Bhakti

This brings us to the practice of *bhakti* as a means of attaining everlasting, superlative Bliss. Since *bhakti* begins with love, and has love of God as the very aim to be achieved, it is blissful from beginning to end. Here, God is the Beloved. He is the most blissful. Even by thinking of our beloved in the world, we are filled with joy. It is natural to expect that by thinking of God, the embodiment of love and bliss, one would be filled with much greater and deeper joy. To know that the Lord is dearer than the dearest, nearer than the nearest, and loves us more than anyone else, fills us with great joy. Others may fail or may abandon us, but the Lord will never do so. Mortals are weak; but the Lord is free from blemishes, and is immortal. To feel the presence of The Beloved is a source of great joy and bliss. Since the impure, uncultured, and crude mind seeks name and form, and sense pleasures, why not give it the sweet name of God and his blissful form to meditate upon? As the mind goes on becoming purer and purer by thinking of God with form, and taking his holy name, it will be able to derive greater and greater bliss, even without the help of name and form. Let us replace *vishayananda*, joy of sense enjoyment, with *bhajanananda*, the joy of singing the glories of God, and this will lead us to *Brahmananda* — the joy of union with God.

> "The mind may become quiet on listening to a sweet melody, or on seeing beautiful, natural scenery. Gazing at the tranquil ocean or the sky may quieten the mind. These states of quietness are technically called *tushnim sthiti* in Vedanta, and adepts recommend that one must not allow these precious moments to pass by unnoticed. One must recognize them and try to remain in them as long as possible."

Bliss Through the Analysis of a King's Happiness

Among worldly happinesses, the happiness of a monarch is the greatest. Why? Because all the lesser worldly joys and pleasures are included in it. What does it mean? A child plays with his dolls and toys. He gets great joy in his play. But as he grows, he puts aside those toys, because the joy which he gets as a grown up supersedes the joy of childhood. Even if a person has not played all the games of childhood, he does not aspire to enjoy them on becoming an adult. Similarly, an emperor does not aspire for the enjoyments of his minister, or of a rich man in his kingdom. In other words, his joy is inclusive of all lower joys. But unfortunately, he too is not satisfied and aspires for higher forms of enjoyments — like those of *gandharvas* and gods.

Now, is it possible to attain the state of non-aspiration for lower joys of a monarch minus the hankering for higher ones, without having to go through the botheration of acquiring and protecting a kingdom? The scriptures say that this can be done by being desireless, and by imbibing the spirit of the scriptures. It is not at all necessary to satisfy all our desires to become absolutely desireless. As a matter of fact, desires are innumerable, and no one can, even in millions of lives, satisfy all his desires, for they go on multiplying and are never quenched by enjoyment. Besides, in an attempt to satisfy our desires we tend to repeat the experience of desire-based-enjoyments over and over again, thus wasting a lot of time and psychic energy. Desires can be overcome only through discrimination. They can be renounced mentally by analyzing their transitory, degrading, binding, and enslaving nature. An absolutely desireless sage is the emperor of emperors, the god of gods, and the most blessed person. He has nothing to fear.

Bliss Through the Analysis of a Child's Bliss

A child enjoys the purest bliss. He has no worries or anxieties for the future, nor is he burdened by the haunting guilt of evil deeds committed in the past. He has neither love nor hatred, attachment nor aversion. His needs are few and he revels in his own self. But unfortunately he is helplessly dependent on others, and as he grows he becomes more and more aware of his utter helplessness, limitations, and insecurity. If one can, like a child, become free from aversion and attachment, likes and dislikes and be free from the bonds of the three *gunas*, without the feeling of helplessness, one can attain supreme bliss. One of the techniques to do this is to be with children, observe them, and impose upon oneself the attitude of a child. Let us try to think that we are the children of God, fully dependent on Him. He is our mother and father, and we have nothing to worry over. In the present age Sri Ramakrishna has clearly demonstrated and advocated this technique.

Bliss Through the Path of Knowledge

Attainment of superlative bliss is possible also through the path of knowledge, *Jnana Yoga*. Supreme blessedness and fulfillment in life can be attained by directly experiencing the fact that one is ever blissful, eternal, and of pure consciousness. Hence one knows, through discrimination, one's blissful Self.

We love many things: our body, wealth, son, wife, friends, etc. But whom do we love most? It is a law that the entity nearest to us is the most beloved. When the son falls ill, one does not hesitate to spend money, however dear it might be. But if the son were to attack, one saves one's body, for it is nearer and dearer than the son. If someone were to try to injure one's senses, like the eyes, one would protect the eyes by covering it with the hand, in spite of the possibility of injuring the hand. It means that the senses are dearer to us than the physical body. But life is even dearer than the senses. We might sacrifice a sense, if required, to save our life, if it is threatened by a disease. But there are people who sacrifice even their lives for certain principles and ideals, which shows that mind is dearer than even life. Thus we find that the entity which is closer to our innermost Self is dearer than the ones distant from it. And since the Atman is the innermost, it is the dearest. The experience of men of realization also proves this. Since that which is dearest gives maximum happiness and vice-versa, the *Atman* is the repository of superlative bliss. This is the process of discrimination for attaining the bliss of the Self.

Bliss Through Serving and Loving Others

One of the best ways of obtaining bliss is to love and serve others. The scriptures say: *"That which is limitless is bliss; there is no happiness in the little, in the limited."* A person marries and becomes two. His bliss increases. He begets children and his family expands. His bliss further increases. It is a common experience that a single, isolated, and alienated person is never happy. By service, we identify with others. It breaks our egoistic limitations and makes us expand. We find ourselves among our own people everywhere. To make others our own through love, service, and help, is the method taught by the Holy Mother to attain peace, happiness, and bliss. The day we would actually realize that no one is a stranger, and that all are our own, that day we shall be the happiest. He is the happiest person who actually feels that no one is a stranger, no one is an enemy, and that all are his very own.

> "Let us try to think that we are the children of God, fully dependent on Him. He is our mother and father, and we have nothing to worry over. In the present age Sri Ramakrishna has clearly demonstrated and advocated this technique."

A former editor of the Vedanta Keshari, and previously of the Ramakrishna Mission Home of Service, Swami Brameshananda is a senior monk of the Ramakrishna Order and until recently was the Secretary of the Ramakrishna Mission Ashram in Chandigarh, India. Over the years his writings in Hindi and English have appeared in several journals, including Prabuddha Bharata, Vedanta Keshari, and Nectar of Nondual Truth. He specializes in themes related to Jainism. He is now retired and is living in Varanasi.

Babaji Bob Kindler ◆

NONSEPARATION & ITS PRACTICE
Ananya & Abhyasa Yogas

Ever since the arrival of the precious Advaita Vedanta on the soils of Europe and America due to Swami Vivekananda's presence on earth, a number of schools representing nondualism have sprung up. Along with these have surfaced several misconceptions about this incomparable philosophy of nonseparation, wherein the apparently individualized soul finally recognizes itself as the Supreme Soul in *"I and my Father are One"* fashion. This is accomplished here on earth, in the physical body, through a sincere and long-standing practice that bases its efforts upon following the spiritual tradition connected to nonduality. One of the aforementioned misconceptions, then, is that though the Supreme Self (Atman) is pure and perfect at all times, beyond time, the unguided, unschooled practitioner falls into the premature assumption that he/she is already That, prior to affirming the fact via spiritual disciplines.

In the Bhagavad Gita, Sri Krishna, *Avatar* and Archetypical Soul, has singled out the yogas of *Ananya* and *Abhyasa* for Arjuna's consideration. *Ananya* refers to the naturally indivisible nature of Consciousness, and *Abhyasa* indicates *"the yoga of constant practice"* through which the embodied soul (*jiva*), living amidst the vagaries and vicissitudes of *maya*, remains in acknowledgement and remembrance of its nondual Essence (*svarupa*). Nonduality, termed *Advaita* in India, applies at all levels of existence, and to all subjects. The *Advaita* of literature and grammar, for instance, demands that we compartmentalize the subject only for the sake of study, not for the purpose of separation, for like the depths of an ocean and its surface, everything abides eternally in a homogenous condition, despite apparent or seeming divisions or contradictions.

Adhering to this universal rule of thumb, the seers know that nonseparation and its practice are nondifferent. This is *Advaita Vedanta Sadhana*. As my guru used to describe it, *"a bird cannot fly without two wings."* Put in another way, grace (*ananya*) and self-effort (*sadhana*) are the same thing, and those who think otherwise simply have not, as yet, engaged in and completed any delusion-shattering discipline that proves this point. The forty days and forty nights in the wilderness undergone by Jesus, the forty-nine days and nights under the Bodhi tree spent by Lord Buddha, the twenty-one days on the mount which Mohammed engaged in — these are fitting examples of intense delusion-dissolving disciplines. After applying and consummating such necessary austerities, these great souls went on practicing, even after enlightenment. Why? For two reasons: first, to be an example for others of what a great effort it takes to walk the *"razor's-edged path"* of spiritual life; and two, to *"keep the mirror of the mind wiped clean"* so as to allow perception of nondual Reality (*Brahman*, Buddha-Nature, Allah, All-Mighty Father, etc.) at its purest level, as Shankara put it.

All of this not only clears up present day thinking on these several crucial points, but also reveals the short-sightedness and, sometimes, the outright hypocrisy of certain contemporary movements and their adherents. Towards this superlative end, Swami Vivekananda stated in his letters, written after visiting America back in the late 1800's, that:

"In America, many movements are struggling for mastery. All of these represent Advaita thought more or less, and that sect which is spreading most rapidly, approaches nearer to it than any of the others. Now, if anything was ever clear to me, it is that one of these must survive, swallowing up all the rest, to be the power of the future. Which is it to be?

"Referring to history, we see that only that fragment which is fit will survive, and what makes it fit to survive but character? Advaita will be the future religion of thinking humanity. No doubt of that. And of all the sects, they alone shall gain the day who are able to show character in their lives — no matter how far along they may be."

Self-Effort is Grace

Character, as Sri Sarada Devi related it to us in the early 1900's, is built upon self-effort, and is the result of intense striving for *dharmic* life, for spiritual life. To put it succinctly, it is not wise to cause a schism between nonduality and self-effort. With poorly thought statements such as "You are God," and "You are already perfect and you do not have to do anything," quasi-nondualists of the day are misleading those who, over many lifetimes of slow growth and gradual advancement, are beginning to gain an interest in things authentically spiritual. And whereas the *krama-mukti* path of gradual enlightenment may not suit the strict nondualist, it is nevertheless the practical approach for those who, as yet, are busy engendering the necessary qualifications for *dharmic* existence, spiritual life, and nondual abidance.

The truth is that time-honored wisdom traditions have always accented the need for striving souls to pierce through veils and overlays. These "false superimpositions" (*vivarta*), as Vedanta cites them, are of differing densities and exist at various levels of consciousness — limitations like the five elements, bodies (name and form), emotions, mental projections, ego, thought, and even cosmic beings and causal regions lying deep within the mind/soul. Failing to see through these perplexing overlays amounts to a decided lack of discernment as far as spiritual teachers are concerned, and demonstrates a sharp line of demarcation between beginning and advanced levels of seekers. Therefore, beginners who are new to the spiritual path, and those who are only pretending to know, are prematurely assuming qualities, character, and conscious stations that are far

> "Whether one calls it *Ashtangika Marga*, *Ashtanga Yoga*, *Sadhanachatushtaya*, or *Abhyasa Yoga* as referred to in this article, it all verily leads to *Ananya* — the Yoga of Nonseparation. Plainly, the *Yoga* of Nonseparation requires the *Yoga* of Constant Practice to both secure and maintain it."

beyond their modest attainment and present reach. To pose perfection before truth-confirming *sadhana* and actual spiritual experience have been attained not only moves to compromise the authenticity of nonduality, it also presents a poor example of it to aspiring humanity.

Delusion Destroying Discipline

When Lord Buddha attained the unattainable through His tremendous self-effort, He declared: *"O architect of this universe, I have seen thee. I will henceforth refrain from creating bodies out of ignorance, whether made of wood, or of stone, or of flesh and bone, or even of wise conception."* Top-level realizations of this highest Goal (*Paragatam*) are not gained by pretension and posturing. Rather, they are the result of a well-planned (study), well-guided (*guru*), well-actuated (*sadhana*), and well-consummated (transcendence) regimen of spiritual practice. Whether one calls it *Ashtangika Marga*, *Ashtanga Yoga*, *Sadhanachatushtaya*, or *Abhyasa Yoga* as referred to in this article, it all verily leads to *Ananya* — the Yoga of Nonseparation. Plainly, the *Yoga* of Nonseparation requires the *Yoga* of Constant Practice to both secure and maintain it.

Happily, all present-day misconceptions around this subject, lying at the intellectual and philosophical levels of the collective and individual mind of humanity, can be done away with completely through one-pointed practice, leaving the soul in peace and in bliss, and in rapt possession of the Self, or Soul. As the *Tathagata* has said, as recorded in the Dhammapada, *"The Self is master of the self; who else would the master be?"* The advaitic axiom of Advaita Vedanta, *Sarvam Khalvidam Brahman* — *"All is Brahman,"* explains this nicely. This radical nondual statement sports a certain complexity which virtually begs for contemplative scrutiny which, when satisfied, then leads to deeper comprehension at both philosophical and intellectual levels.

Are Name and Form Brahman?

Upon close internal inspection — as *tattvas* in Sankhya, *nidanas* in Buddhism, *alambanas* in Yoga, *vivarta* (false superimpositions) in Vedanta, and *abhavapadarthas* in Advaita Vedanta — forms are not *Brahman*. And as we know, what to speak of forms, at least four of the major religious traditions of the world will not accept any name for Divine Reality. Decidedly, as well, anything that appears in space, that experiences cause and effect, or, under the strictest measure, undergoes transformation (as in birth, growth, disease, decay, old age, and death) of any kind, cannot be included within that singular and superlative category that Indian *Darshanas* term *Brahman*, either (see chart on *Aparinama*, nontransformation, on the facing page.

How is it, then, that the statement *"All is Brahman"* can be duly applied to all that we see, taste, touch, hear, and smell, and to objects in relativity? If nature cannot form God, if the seers will not venture to name God, and if the five levels of space (*akashas*) cannot hold God, what is the secret to such a nondual utterance by realized souls? The secret lies in the fact that all of these factors — elements, objects, senses, subtle objects, subtle senses, mind, intellect, and ego — are "*Ananya*," and are not to be separated from Reality in the first place. If these principles are mistakenly assumed to be outside of Reality, only then can they be singled out by such assignments as "unreal," "illusory," "transitory," and "ephemeral." But if these selfsame principles are affirmed to be within the sweep of Reality, lying under the what is singularly all-pervasive" (*vyapti*), then a philosophical fingernail-hold can be afforded through which the mind can comprehend the subtlemost route up the steep mountain-face of cohesive practice to arrive at that superlative Goal which is the distant peak of nondual realization. To make this all exceedingly simple, and in Swami Vivekananda's words, *"God is not in the world; the world is in God."* From this radical nondual station, form is Formlessness, nature is Natural, names infer Existence, and the seven worlds/*chakras* are full of nothing other than the all-abiding Presence of Brahman.

Green Coconut Oneness

Another tact, from a different direction, can be borrowed in this regard to allow for comprehension of the potentially flummoxing maxim (*i.e.*, *the Mahavakya of "All Is Brahman"*) presently under scrutiny. There is no doubt that, from the standpoint of inexperienced souls entering into various spiritual arenas, all objects, pleasures, desires, and things, are God to them — or are their gods. In this way, these as yet inexperienced souls claim, prematurely, that *"All is Brahman."* This is what Sri Ramakrishna has called *"green coconut oneness."* That is, when the coconut is unripe it is all one solid mass, but when it ripens it turns into five layers (outer shell, inner shell, husk, meat, and milk). His inference is that when the mind of the aspirant is still unripe, or green, he/she projects a kind of immature "oneness" over everything, never even imagining that there are really five layers, called relativity or maya, in that projection.

Over millennia, various complementary philosophical systems of India have perceptively (and ingeniously) presented these sets of fives as different types of quintuplication processes, i.e., the Five *Koshas* of Vedanta, the Five *Akashas* of Vasishtha's Yoga, the five sets of Five *Tattvas* (if one counts *Mahat* in with the *Antahkarana*) of Kapila's Sankhya Yoga, the Five *Kleshas* of Patanjali's Yoga, and various sets of fives in Buddhism and Jainism as well. Seeing through these projections of the mind — not only on the individual level but at the subtler stage of col-

Aparinama — The Principle of Nontransformation

"A kind of scientific advaitism has been spreading throughout Europe ever since the theory of the conservation of energy was discovered. But all that is Parinama, evolution by real modification, as contrasted to Aparinama, progressive manifestation by unreal superimposition. Ramanuja's theory is that the bound soul has its perfections involved, and when this perfection evolves it becomes free. But the Advaitan declares that involution and evolution take place only in show. Both processes are in Maya, and so are apparent only." — **Swami** Vivekananda

"All happenings taking place in relativity resemble the activities of a man running a race in a dream. Nothing actually transpires. Scenery, movements, race, dream — all are unreal, or apparent only. The dreamer alone is real, but he must awaken to realize this." — Gaudapada

Brahman
Paramatman
The Nontransformational Reality

Pratyagatman
Antaryami
Kutastha
Sakshi
Aum

"The unreal has no existence; the Real never ceases to be. The truth about both has been realized by the seers. Coming into being and ceasing to be do not take place in the Absolute. It is unborn, eternal, constant and timeless." — Sri Krishna

Aparinama
Nontransformation

Parinama
Apparent Transformation

Maya — name, form, time, space, causation
Prakrti — manifest and unmanifested nature

"Though knowledge, being a compound, cannot be the Absolute itself, it is the nearest approach to it, and higher than will or desire."

INTELLIGENCE / KNOWLEDGE
(Sattva)

- Chidabhasa — Pure Intelligence reflecting off of Reality
- Anubhava — Direct Perception of Reality
- Paravidya — Sacred Wisdom of the Nondual Scriptures
- Upalabdhi — Insight via Divine Remembrance

"The Divine first becomes knowledge, then, in the second degree that of will."

MIND / WILL
(Rajas)

- Abhijna — Intuition
- Ahamkara — Sense of separate "I"-ness
- Ahamta-vrtti — Self-arrogating Thought
- Aparavidya — Secular Intelligence

"If it is, this is the evolution, less and less in the body and more and more in the mind — man the highest form, meaning manas, thought — the animal that thinks, and not the animal that senses only."

BRAIN / SENSES / DESIRE
(Tamas)

- Indriyajnana — Sense-knowledge / Sense-perception
- Vedana — Feelings / Sensations from Contact with Objects
- Vasana — Desires based in Past Experiences

"So long as the upadhis are present, the jivas retain their individuation. But the Paramatman undergoes no change due to these superimpositions. As the clay pot is not a transformation of the unchanging akasha, so too the jiva is not a transformation of the immutable Paramatman, who had these changes projected upon It by ignorant minds." — Gaudapada

lective and cosmic Mind as well — constitutes true perception. As Jesus put it, *"If thine eye be single thou shalt know the Truth."* Videlicet, the mental *sadhana* of seeing through appearances is crucial for the ongoing perception of Nondual Reality.

King Viveka

Here, then, is discrimination, or *viveka*, as it is termed in Vedanta. It is discernment of a rare type, at a very subtle level, and it is missing in most beings, even spiritual aspirants, in this, the *Kali Yuga*. When the discriminating seeker espies and secures real *viveka*, it is then and only then that "green coconut oneness" becomes a thing of the past, and true oneness, *Ananya*, comes to the fore. As Sri Ramachandra has stated in the Adhyatma Ramayana, *"Enlightenment dawns on the mind in stages."* In other words, the sense of this sublime oneness matures in the human mind over time — as long as it engages itself in spiritual practice, *Abhyasa Yoga*.

This is dependent on the timely acquisition of the quality of *viveka*. Where does it hail from? It springs from constant attendance on the atmosphere of holy beings, itself the result of the yearning for perfection through constant practice over lifetimes. It is termed "holy company" by Lord Vasishtha, and is one of the great Four Sentinels of Spiritual Life. Satisfying this requisite, the maturing aspirant weeds out names, forms, objects, and things via the mind's well-honed discernment since they are, at his or her maturing state of awareness, obviously not the formless, nameless, objectless Reality. This auspicious process (*neti neti*) eventually carries the mind beyond quotients, lists, and multiples, into a homogenous state. Here, in the transcendent atmosphere of nonduality, Reality cannot be adequately explained in terms of numerical oneness; It must be affirmed as all-pervasive oneness, as "not-two." It is now realized as It always was and ever is, as preeminently natural and spontaneous — as *Ananya*.

Know Thyself, On All Levels

To the impatient soul, and to all those who attempt progress by jumping steps, an old story can be offered for consideration. If one has strong legs, as Sri Ramakrishna has said, one may jump from the lowest step to the highest step of a staircase. But after such an impetuous move, doubt may set in as to what the middle steps consist of. On the other hand, the wise student who navigates a step at a time, examining everything along the way, will know that the middle steps are made of the same ingredients, i.e., brick, lime dust, etc., as the upper and lower steps. Thus, no backtracking will be necessary later, on down the path.

This simple story applies well to the subject of practice and nonduality. It is not that *Advaita/Ananya*/Nonduality/Reality is completely devoid of name, form, and objects. It is more that name, form, and objects are all potential there, especially if one takes into consideration great intermediary principles like AUM, Unmanifested *Prakriti*, and *Mahat*. Such refined knowledge makes for a much more comprehensive philosophical standpoint for the embodied being. Pertinent to practice, *abhyasa*, the impatient seeker is like a fruit stand owner who sells only the meat of the fruit, throwing the rest away. But the knower of Truth is like an experienced fruit merchant who places the entire fruit on the scale to get its proper weight, then sells the flesh only after feeding the core and peelings to the cows and keeping the seeds for future harvest.

To "flesh" out this all-inclusive philosophy at the cosmological level is to reveal the need for the "practitioner" to live up to his name. It is said that when Jesus told His apostles about "The Word," they could not comprehend it at first. They had to go to Gethsemane and meditate under the transformative influence of the Master. So, even in those times, it was not practical for the novitiate of spiritual life to say, *"I and my Father are One"* until they had seen and known the building blocks of the inner universe — the *"Kingdom of Heaven within."* A more qualified axiom to follow would have been *"Be thee perfect as the Father in Heaven is perfect."*

In other words, rivers, nets, fish, wives, children, and huts are all well and good as far as the outer world and its institutions are concerned, but in order to get divested of Mammon, invested with Divinity, and become *"fishers of men,"* the soul must perceive all that is within the Great Mind (*Mahat*) and its radiant regions. Called *"lokas"* in Sanskrit, these inner worlds represent a major portion of the penultimate station of God with form. Knowledge of these internal chambers of consciousness confers a substantial and essential bulk of understanding upon the human mind attempting to reach the ultimately enlightened state of Nonduality.

Chambers, Chakras, and the Chosen Ideal

The Indian *Darshanas* of Sankhya, Vedanta, and Yoga ask the practitioner of *dharma* to meditate on all the supports of the multifaceted universes of name and form, from the five elements of this physical realm (*mahabhutas* in *jagrat*) on through to the

> *"Pertinent to practice, abhyasa, the impatient seeker is like a fruit stand owner who sells only the meat of the fruit, throwing the rest away. But the knower of Truth is like an experienced fruit merchant who places the entire fruit on the scale to get its proper weight, then sells the flesh only after feeding the core and peelings to the cows and keeping the seeds for future harvest."*

Ajativada: Nonorigination

"Atman, the Indivisible Soul of mankind, is unborn. It does not pass in and out of existence; It is Existence! This truth is discovered in Consciousness as an eternal Verity. This is not a matter of going inside or outside; the Infinite Brahman can never be realized through the finite universe. Mind and matter are neither destructible nor indestructible. They are unoriginated." Swami Aseshananda

Incomplete Theories about the Soul & Creation:

The Will of the Lord
The Work of Time & Space
For the Sake of Enjoyment
For Sportive Play (Lila)

Truth about the Soul & Creation:

It is Unborn
It is Free of Sleep
It is Devoid of Dreams
It is Free of Names and Forms
It is Spontaneous, Immediate
It is Omniscient
It is Free of Conceptualization
It is Intense Concentration without end

Brahman
Moksha
Mukti
Formlessness
Transcendence
Awareness
Nirvikalpa
Chaitanya
Kaivalya
Nirvana
Satori

"Mind and entities are traditionally known as free of creation and destruction. Those who know this do not fall into error. When the dreaming mind vibrates it gives rise to the two and the many, but when it is free of all cause and effect it remains unoriginated." Gaudapada

Embodied soul departing time & space

"All is One, unborn, tranquil, endless, certain, immutable. See Reality as Spirit; be even-minded and at ease. This is the state through which you will become liberated, even while inhabiting a body."
Akshi Upanisad

subtle elements of the dream state (*tanmatras* in *svapna*), and even deeper into the formless level of deep sleep (causal seeds/*bijams* in *sushupti*). The latter two of these three states of mankind's consciousness represent the middle steps of the "Great Staircase" leading up and through the internal worlds of subtle name and form — what Jesus referred to when He said *"My Father's Mansion has many Chambers."* Kundalini Yoga speaks of these chambers of consciousness in terms of seven *Chakras*, or Lotuses, which are internal vortexes of gradated awareness. Through inward ascension the aspiring soul contacts and connects with them, finally meeting its "chosen Ideal," *Ishvara*, the most profound form of Consciousness. This definitive communion is called *"....getting to the Father through the Son,"* in Christianity, and is highly advised along that precipitous ascent into nondual Awareness. Expressed in practical terms, one needs friends in high places, and there is no better friend than the "Eternal Companion," the last vestige of form the inward ascending soul will encounter on the spiritual journey — what the ancient *rishis* of India called *"The Flight of the Alone to the Alone in the Upanisads*.

Sadhana and Samskaras

Along the winsome way of spiritual practice, or *sadhana*, many hidden imperfections are rooted out of the mind, mental residue that collected and got projected over previous lifetimes. These impressions (*samskaras*) of good, bad, and mixed experiences accumulated due to constant relations with nature, with objects, and with worlds — what to speak of with other souls who were mutually dreaming the dream of name and form in space and time. Many so-called births and deaths — so-called because the real Soul, *Atman*, is birthless and deathless (see the chart on *Ajativada*, Nonorigination, on the previous page) — were undergone over an infinite sweep of time. Memories of fearful experiences thus got stored in the mind's memory. These will not only come forth during life, and at the time of death, but may emerge in the present existence as the aspirant attempts to transcend the worlds of name and form in meditation.

Further, if fear of nature, of the elements such as earth, fire, and water comes up, for instance, it is because the soul had painful relations with the likes of earthquakes and landslides, housefires and forestfires, and floods and drownings. The fear he holds due to such experiences will counteract his attempts towards spiritual growth. Only knowledge will get rid of that fear, for to know a thing allows one to master it. That is why Sri Krishna states in the Bhagavad Gita, *"In all the worlds, knowledge is the greatest purifier."* For this reason, and for all those listed above, the practitioner is to engage in meditation on God with form to prepare the soul for nondual realization.

Pleasures in Paradise

Other facts cannot be left out of this rendering either, such as the enjoyments of pleasure in nature, and with the elements, causing attachment to the world and forgetfulness of one's essential Consciousness (*chaitanya*) that is beyond nature. As Sri Ramakrishna has stated, *"The more that the soul reincarnates in the physical body in ignorance, the more it begins to believe that the world is real."* In this wise, the sincere practitioner is advised by the illumined *guru* to learn the spiritual arts of detachment and austerity, rather than to fall complacently into the ever-ready traps of sensual enjoyments, heaven-seeking, and intellectual pursuits. Bondage to nature and convention is the result of this fall, while freedom to the mind leading to realization of the ever-free *Atman* is the welcome alternative.

Parting Shots

To conclude, the student and teacher, both, should never be bereft of spiritual practice. Until full realization dawns, both must refrain from saying, thinking, or teaching that the embodied being is perfect and need do nothing for his or her realization. Whereas it is true that Divine Reality is ever pure and perfect, the embodied soul (body/mind mechanism) is far from it, and will not realize this internal and eternal perfection until the mind is purified by spiritual practice.

In short, and as was once told to me by an illumined soul, *"You are not Brahman until you realize you are Brahman."* In the meantime, the question may be asked, what is life for if not for fulfilling the saying, "practice makes perfect?"

Further, for the enlightened soul, this art of practice will strengthen and expand the quality of forbearance, which is the most preferable default zone for the realized being occupying the embodied state here in the world. This also ushers in the birth of true compassion, where the Yoga of Nonseparation, The Yoga of Constant Practice, and the Art of Selfless Service all meet and commingle to express a consummate yoga for this Age.

Babaji Bob Kindler is the Spiritual Director of the SRV Associations with centers in Hawaii, Oregon, and California. A teacher of religion and spirituality and a prolific author, his books include *The Avadhut, Twenty-Four Aspects of Mother Kali, Ten Divine Articles of Sri Durga, Sri Sarada Vijnanagita, Swami Vivekananda Vijnanagita, An Extensive Anthology of Sri Ramakrishna's Stories, A Quintessential Yoga Vasishtha, Reclaiming Kundalini Yoga, and others*. Founder and Artistic Director of Jai Ma Music, he is also an accomplished musician and composer who has produced over twenty-five albums of instrumental and devotional music to date.

Swami Aseshananda

TEACHINGS FROM THE KATHO UPANISAD

This class in a series on the Katho Upanisad was given in the 1980's by Swami Aseshanandaji Maharaj around Christmas time at the Vedanta Society of Portland. No other recordings of this series are available. In this class the swami begins at part 2 of the scripture.

Today we shall study the Upanisad called the Katho Upanisad. As this study goes on over weeks the number of people attending and listening will become fewer and fewer. That is because this country has selected the *bhogamarga* as the path of life. And this path of enjoyment is fraught with fear, fraught with insecurity, and courts the meaninglessness of life. Thus, the Vedanta philosophy tells the Western countries to try and halt this madness for enjoyment attended by this madness for power, because this madness for the sensate pleasures of life will spell disaster in the end.

You might say that this message is negative, but negative things are necessary at first. There is darkness. What do you do? You have to inform people that they are quite happy in darkness, with Christmas celebrations, with giving of gifts and with festivities and frolic. I can tell you, that when this merriment comes based upon "Merry Christmas," if I had had any say or power I would have changed that saying. [laughter] "Merry Christmas" has little to do with the Christ. Life in Jesus is not for merriment, or power, or war. Life in Christ is spiritual life, and that life means renunciation. You see, people may call themselves Christians, but they have not accepted the real Christ. In order to accept Christ you have to follow the spiritual path, not the *bhogamarga*, the path of enjoyment. Nor also the *pravrittimarga*, thinking the practicalities of life to be real and paramount.

The Western civilization has based their lives on the fallacy that the world is real. They are called realists; they are practical people. But really, I find that they are the most impractical people, because the world is changeful; therefore it is not real. The Real is always and ever Changeless; India has known that to be the case for millennia.

Thus, a part of the theme of this Upanisad is blame. We try to blame people for the world's problems, or we assign the blame to God. Why has He made this world so changeful? Why, as the Upanisad says, has He *"made the senses outgoing only?" (IV:1)* Just to deliver you a little bit of sensation? [laughter] Or excitement?

The Old Witch, the World

Everywhere you go in this old witch, the world, you find that society is secular. Everywhere you go! Only a few people are spiritually awakened. And how does one become spiritual? *Anityam asukham*, as Krishna states in the Gita. By knowing that the world is transitory and devoid of real happiness; or at least ephemeral. That was the case with the Buddha. He was awakened. He was awakened when he saw that there was disease, that there was old age, that there was death. And then He asked this question. Will it happen to me? Yes! It will happen to you, and to your son, Rahula. Then He realized *sarvadukha, sarvanitya* — true happiness and spiritual realization. So you see, it is not pessimism. Nor is it realism or pragmatism only. It is only turning the mind to another kind of life.

And so, the Katho Upanisad relates in today's verse about *bala. [IV:2] Bala* here means children. Children means immature persons. Essentially, it means those who are not lighting and using the torch of discrimination, *viveka*. And it is in the prior verse that the *rishi* tells that the senses have been created to look outwards only. The eyes thrill at the sight of Christmas lights; houses bedecked with such outer grandeur that your neighbor becomes jealous. [laughter] But who wants to see the inner Light? They follow *"kaman" (IV:2)* the verse states here. *Kaman* means outer enjoyments for the sense objects of the world.

And this is called the *Pravrittimarg*. That path is always moving towards the false idea of evolution, towards the periphery and away from the center, towards the vision of *trishna*. That means thirst. They have got thirst for surface enjoyments. It is desire, and if you have one you want another. It is television, not God-vision. [laughter] If you have a television, then you want a color television. Then you must have one for your wife, another for grownup youth, and another for the young ones, called kids. [laughter] Then you must have one in the basement. [more laughter]

And this is the outer light of television. With television you look always towards the outer light, towards the hypnotizing periphery, but in God-vision you get finely focused on the center. With no discrimination people are like children, *balam*. They follow the senses outwards. You see, it is not only Sri Ramakrishna who saw old men playing with cards, with nothing else to do; I have also seen them here in the West. Nothing else to do but shuffle their feet as they walk towards the gaming table to shuffle cards. [laughter] Just today I met one woman who said she cannot come to class because of a competition. Some champion had come to town, you see. So, these are people who have nothing to do; nothing to do. They are wasting their time. So they join a knitting circle, or an old man's club. [laughter]

But one young girl came to me who wanted to know how to meditate. This is a sign of a higher path, a higher desire. The *Bhogamarga* is the path of lower desire, of thirst. And that type of desire cannot be quenched. *"Vanity of vanities, all this is vanity."* But still people will not learn.

Desire is Death

And so, next, the Upanisad states that these children, *"they follow the wide-spreading snare of death." (IV:2)* It is like a fisherman's net; the larger the net, the more the fish. The Sanskrit word here is *vasana*, desire; desire is death. From a spiritual man's point of view, this is the case. The multiplication of desires which you call progress is all about moving towards death. So renounce all desires and keep only one desire before you. "I will attain freedom from death." And attain immortality. Yes, that is the idea: immortality is the main theme here. I have read, that when the cattle are taken to the slaughter house, there is one of them that leads; the others follow. He is a bit clever, you see. But he is the lamb that leads others to the slaughter. Among people we call that lamb Judas. It is very unfortunate.

Now, this *sloka* also takes a more exceptional person into account. The Sanskrit word utilized here is *"dhira."* (IV:1) *Dhira* means steady, a steady-minded person. The head must be cool and calm, you see. But very often what happens is that the head becomes warm, even hot. [laughter] Why? Because of the passions.

There are six passions. They are to be controlled.....under your control. *Kama, krodha, lobha, moha, mada, matsarya*. In English you know them well. They are lust, anger, greed, infatuation, pride/vanity, and jealousy. But their leader, the Judas among them [laughter], is desire. The passions could be described as controllable, but desire is intrinsically bad.

snares of death. Those who seek this way are *vivekis*; they use their discrimination in life. The Upanisads also call them *"vira."* They are noble, like heros. Shankara says that you are to test your powers of discrimination, and use *vichar*. Always ask, "Will this help me to realize the Truth?"

Otherwise, the Upanisad talks about the man who is not fully realized yet. He is still a *sadhika*. He is an aspirant that has come to know the unreality of the world, but is still unable to fully detach from it. Then he came in contact with a very interesting person. [laughter] Intellectually he has understood that the supreme goal of life is to conquer death. And this is not only intellectual, he is now convinced that he must follow the path to perfection. He thinks, "I have followed the path of *preyas* and found it bitter and disappointing. Now I must follow the path of *shreyas* and attain immortality.

This path of *shreyas* includes the path of *dharma*. You cannot attain immortality without the path of *dharma*. Righteous living is necessary. In dharmic life, you see, he will read the scriptures and will hear the Truth from an illumined teacher.

So how does spiritual realization come? The Upanisad now mentions *druvam*. (IV:2) Since everything changes constantly in this world of flux, one finds not only nowhere to lay his head,

> *"In this world of flux one finds not only nowhere to lay his head, he cannot even find a place to hang his hat. He finds the world hollow and vacant. It has no permanent basis in Reality. Faced with all this, then, he perceives that which is druvam; that which is permanent, that which is stable, that which is secure. At this point he is on the path of detachment leading to renunciation."*

Really, man is born to cultivate the stance of deathlessness. That is why you are born, to conquer death. But man forgets due to *avidya*, ignorance of his true nature — Atman. And *avidya* leads to *karma*. And *karma* creates *samskaras*. *Samskaras*, mental impressions due to desires enjoyed and suffered in a previous lifetime, hems them in. It is like the fence that keeps the cattle from seeking their freedom. Buddha called this craving. Now, Vedantists call this *vasana*, desire. Holy Mother said that this world is going on, and has been created, due to *vasanas*. Every person contributes his or her *vasanas* into the mixture. Some like food; they like to eat food. If they feel weighted down by this, both in body and in mind, they will exercise another method. That is called diet. [laughter] And jogging. [swami laughs, and all laugh] But these will not lessen the weight.

So, here it is the palate-desire. You see, one very large person came to me and wanted to follow. I told her, "If you want to follow, then for now don't take butter; don't take cream; don't take pastry." She looked at me in shock and said, "But swami, then what is this life for?" [long period of laughter]

Holy Company is for the Righteous

So you see, there is *satsangha*, and that is a type of desire too. The illumined souls will be there for you in what is called "holy company" to answer your questions around spiritual matters. But there the desire is for *jivanmukti*, the desire for freedom from the

he cannot even find a place to hang his hat [laughter]. He finds the world hollow and vacant. It has no permanent basis in Reality. Faced with all this, then, he perceives that which is *druvam*; that which is permanent, that which is stable, that which is secure. At this point he is on the path of detachment leading to renunciation. And the path of meditation. This leads to the path of the Eternal. He now thinks in terms of crossing the *samsaric* seas of time, space, and causation. For, all that is experienced in these three oceans in not permanent; it will not last.

Then, finally, he finds himself firmly situated on the path of renunciation. The Upanisad states, then: *"Only by following the path of renunciation, some discriminating persons have found themselves free from death."*

Another point about *druvam*, what is permanent, is that those who attain it do not seek heaven. Heaven is not an unshakable immortality; it is a relative immortality only. For a certain time you may enjoy the benefits of that world. They are gained by *karmaphala*. By good deeds you can go to heaven. But heaven belongs to time and is the effect of a cause. Therefore it cannot be permanent. When Christ talked about Heaven, he specified that it was within, and called that state *"I and my Father are One."* That is the experience of *Advaita*, nonduality.

What transcends the journey to lower heaven is the will to live a *dharmic* life and strengthen one's character, all on a solid foundation. Then the mind gets attracted to the Ultimate. It thinks, "No more pennies from heaven for me." [laughter]

Meditation, Light, and Samadhi

And so, the Upanisad focuses in on realization. The path of *shreyas* becomes desirable to the aspiring soul searching for the Supreme Goal. And so he goes to a teacher and gets a mantra, and meditates upon the meaning of the mantra. Then he will not give up spiritual life until the goal is reached. Here in the West, you see, you do not understand the guru principle. You betray yourself, forsake your teacher, and give up the mantra — all due to some ruse, or some excuse. Or you think you can run here and there and take many teachers and multiple mantras. This is all restlessness and folly. Therefore, Swami Abedhananda has sung, in his hymn to Holy Mother, *"O Mother, do thou this day save thy children caught in maya's chains, full of blemishes and ever vain."*

The mantri guru gives guidance, guidance with regards to what path one should follow. The guru gives the suggestion, but the person himself will have to accept it. If he cannot, then he has not yet practiced and mastered *pratyahara*. *Pratyahara* means withdrawal of the mind from the sense objects of the world. Next come *dharana*, and that is the first stage of real meditation. It is not possible without *pratyahara*. *Pratyahara* amounts to "I can enjoy, but I will not." This means, if you go to any place, and there is some kind of party, and people tell you that you have to drink, you take a ginger ale. [laughter] It is like saying to people through example, "I am not interested in mundane intoxicants. Your social habits are harmful."

This happened to one swami, you see. They invited him to go to some cocktail party, and surprisingly, he accepted. So they told him, "Be sure to have a drink. It is New York, and that is what they do there. You should not miss it." But he told them later, "No, I missed it. I have missed many of those types of things, and I do not regret it in the least." So, one of the great dangers of the Western world is drink. If I had any power I would close down all drinking in all houses. And religious sentiments in Western houses? Yes, there is a little. But the drinking there far exceeds a little. [laughter]

The *slokas* about *Atman* are verses 3, 4, and 5. (IV:3-5) Real meditation on That is encouraged by listening to the guru's teachings. One gets intellectually convinced by this. Then one is to meditate thereafter. This is not mechanical, such as sitting for hours with a blank mind. You see, these types of meditators have no *mantra* and no knowledge, so they get no success, make no headway. One is to enter into the spiritual meaning of the mantra connected to the *Ishtam*, and that will bear fruit.

Authentic meditation will lead to the highest stage of *Yoga* called *samadhi* — a transcendental state of consciousness where there will not be any duality. There will not be any more distinction between the *jivatman* and the *Paramatman*. The Upanisad mentions *angustham*. (IV:12) This is saying *"the size of a thumb."* This is a reference to the *Atman*. Shankara interprets this reference as a "stick of Light," *Jyoti*. Then, *adhumakah* (IV:13) means smokeless, a smokeless Light. It is a symbol of the real Self of man. You may ask, "How can the real Self of man be the size of a thumb? The real Self is all-pervasive." The "size of a thumb" here means a point of focus; you have to focus within.

According to Patanjali there are two types of meditation. In one, you meditate on the heart of a seer or saint. The other is to meditate on the "Ocean of Sorrowless Light" within you — *Jyotismata*. So, this Light is a "smokeless Light." Smokeless means free of the obscuring haze of ignorance.

Light as Mother

Now, in the books on Yoga you find this is called *Kundalini*, infinite power. But She is asleep. So long as She is asleep we are doing normal activities using the *Ida* and *Pingala*, the two subtle nerves. But the higher centers, called *chakras*, are located along the main nerve channel called the *Sushumna*. The *yogis* meditate upon the highest center. The *jnanis* meditate upon the throat and third eye centers. The *bhaktas* should meditate in the heart. This is not the physiological heart; it is the spiritual heart. In yogic language it is called the *anahata*. At the three lower centers, called *muladhara*, *svadhisthana*, and *manipura*, beings are not thinking of their Chosen Ideal, of God. It is only when She is awake at the heart center that one thinks of the Beloved, the Chosen Ideal. Energy, interest, and enthusiasm — these three things come when you meet Mother at the *anahata*.

So, this verse is about meditation. When you are in the state of real meditation, you are the meditator and the object of meditation. But the goal of meditation is unification of the subject and object. And that is called *Nirvikalpa Samadhi*. In that state of states you witness, as the Upanisad now reads, *Ishanah bhutabhavyasya*, "....the Lord of the past and the future." (IV:12) What does that mean? It is eternal. The Lord here is not lording over the process of time; that is only *Isha*. It is *Atman*. It is the same today, and will be same tomorrow. It is timeless, indivisible.

Shankara here, in his commentary, refutes the materialistic philosophy of life that thinks that when the body dies, everything is finished. There is no soul. Charvaka states that. He states that one should enjoy all the good things of life while the body is alive. For, when the body is cremated and reduced into ashes, what are the chances of its coming back? Shankara states that though the body changes, the Reality is changeless. The Gita says this: "Even in this life, they have conquered death!"

So, death is in the Hindu way of thinking. The Buddhists and the Vedantists, however, think in terms of rebirth. They are not afraid of death, they are afraid of rebirth. For, it is for the fulfillment of desire that man comes back again and again into this world of *maya*. Thus, the Katho Upanisad says that desire is death.

Swami Aseshananda, a direct disciple of Sri Sarada Devi, Sri Ramakrishna's wife and spiritual consort, was the Spiritual Minister of the Vedanta Society of Portland for over forty years. He also received holy company with some of the direct disciples of the Great Master. He is the author of *Glimpses of a Great Soul*, on the life and teachings of Swami Saradananda.

◆ *Brother Tadrupa*

BRAHMACHARYA IN THE MODERN AGE
Teachings, Reflections, Insights, & Suggestions

As far back as Sri Krishna's times, the beneficial attribute of celibacy has been both encouraged and practiced, and it is partly for this reason that the culture of India has recognized its facility in earthly life, but realized its important role in spiritual life as well. In present times, Sri Ramakrishna Paramahamsa has stated that complete sexual abstinence for the monk, and refined moderation for the householder, is the way — even for those who are planning families. In the West, *brahmacharya*, which is one of the five basic practices of preliminary Yoga (*yamas*), is still being taken up (if it is taken up at all) for all the wrong reasons. In the puerile Western mind, the persistent idea of going without sexual fulfillment and stimulation because there is something morally wrong with it, taints the practice and stymies its potentially beneficial results. To store up vital energy to be utilized for purposes of gaining Enlightenment is more the idea, and the energy that is successfully stored up can be helpful in fulfilling ones desires on the earthly plane as well.

Brahmacharya, usually translated into English as continence or celibacy, is lauded throughout the wisdom scriptures of many religious traditions. As Lord Krishna states in the Bhagavad Gita, *"Serene and fearless, firm in the vow of brahmacharya, subdued in mind, he should sit in yoga thinking on Me and intent on Me alone. Keeping himself ever steadfast in this manner, the yogi of subdued mind attains Peace abiding in Me and culminating in Nirvana."*

Modern Sexuality and the Predicament of Today's Youth

Modern spiritual exemplars such as Dalai Lama and Mahatma Gandhi bear testament to the profound impact of mature *brahmacharya*. This indispensable discipline and attainment is often easily misunderstood and overlooked by the Western World with its taboo, rigidity, and sensationalist outlook on sexuality. In ancient India, all students underwent a lengthy period of studying under an illumined spiritual guru while practicing unbroken *brahmacharya*. These pure-minded students obtained vast powers of concentration and sense-mastery. Being firmly established in spiritual principles, they became monks or householders and proceeded towards conclusion of all desires resulting in Self-realization. Each student reached or vastly advanced toward total fulfillment both in the *pravritti* (external) and *nirvritti* (internal, transcendent) aspects of their being. Many became seers of various levels of attainment while supporting and strengthening the fabric of society through selfless service of God dwelling in mankind.

This is a vast contrast from the trajectory and schooling of the present youth of the West. With one's understanding of sexuality derived from materialism with its close affiliate of hedonism, and conventional religion with its puritanical morality, maturing youngsters are often left in a vice of fear-based repression, confusion, ignorance, and excess. This often leads to decades, if not lifetimes, of suffering and bondage due to indiscriminate actions contrary to manifesting one's spiritual nature. Western aspirants need an alternative to these uninformed views, and a method that neutralizes their cumulative effects in the mind. The cultivation of *brahmacharya* is an essential key towards this end. This article will share teachings, reflections, insights, and suggestions gleaned from an ongoing vow of *brahmacharya* in hopes that it may properly convey the necessity and profound benefits of this discipline.

Requisites for Practice

To properly practice *brahmacharya* one should first understand its definition and implications. First, rather than merely celibacy, it is more complete to know it as the practice of dwelling in Brahman i.e., Divine Reality. This Reality is ultimately formless, actionless, nameless, beyond space and time, yet able to express Itself through the Universe. Second, *brahmacharya* is the practice of continuity of an authentic spiritual ideal. As my spiritual teacher, Babaji Bob Kindler, stated in a discourse, *"You are incontinent when you betray your path."*

It follows, then, that practicing *brahmacharya* is about unbroken remembrance of God and using such divine awareness as a discriminative criteria for when actions and thoughts are congruent with one's spiritual Ideal. Thus, to begin this practice, one must have proper spiritual education and sincere dedication to a path. Otherwise, an ignorant and destructive sort of repression of desires may take place.

In my own case, a form of *brahmacharya* began when I was initiated into the path of Vedanta by my guru. This was after years of taking the trouble to consistently attend classes, retreats, and establish a strong correspondence with my spiritual exemplars. After changes in my life circumstances and further instruction and assessment by my teacher, the opportunity to take a formal vow of *brahmacharya* was suggested. I saw this vow as an auspicious occasion to intensify my *sadhana* (spiritual discipline) and eliminate my mind's penchant for sensual distractions, known in Sanskrit as *vasana samskaras*. At the time, I was moving into SRV Associations' ashram in Portland, Oregon. The supportive and pure environment allowed for maximum benefit and fidelity to the commitment. As will be seen, the supports of sincere devotion for a genuine spiritual path and holy company provide the foundation for *brahmacharya*.

> "....I was able to keep the mind continent to higher spiritual principles. My mind developed a double awareness where I could be intently listening and working with others, while simultaneously cognizing that we were really just one self. This gave me conviction that desire is really part of the story told by the mind. By controlling the storyteller, the story itself can shift dramatically."

Early Practice and Insights

The beginning stages of *brahmacharya* has outer and inner components. In the outer component, the practitioner, of course, abstains from all forms of sexual contact. But more importantly, the inner component consists of making a mental effort to avoid all forms of sexual thought. Essentially one is to make thought, word, and deed devoid of all ideas of sex.

In my own experience, the inner aspect has proved to be a difficult, immense, and deeply revealing undertaking. Conducting life's practical affairs and interacting with others while trying to avoid breaking my practice mentally, I at once became aware of how prevalent and excessive sensuality is in America. It was frustratingly impossible to avoid encountering aggravating images, speech, and people with regard to my commitment. On a deeper level, it proved to me how attraction and desire are really the basis of society and the activities of most beings. From these early challenges I realized that the practice of *brahmacharya* is primarily mental, and in the beginning requires an active and constant effort to replace desire-based thought with those centered in the spiritual pursuit. To this end, I found myself employing a variety of techniques which seemed to be based in some of the Four Yogas. The easiest approach, being devotional in nature, was to mentally chant my mantra to Sri Ramakrishna and/or simply think of Him. If an objectionable thought or situation came up, a simple mental judo redirection toward the Lord was quite effective and efficient.

A more intermediate approach to the mental aspect of *brahmacharya*, which developed after some advancement in my meditation practice, was to simply restrain the rising of thoughts (*chitta vrittis*). This was especially helpful when dealing with others. By simply not thinking of beings as having various qualities, or as separate from myself, I was able to keep the mind continent to higher spiritual principles. My mind developed a double awareness where I could be intently listening and working with others, while simultaneously cognizing that we were really just one self. This gave me conviction that desire is really part of the story told by the mind. By controlling the storyteller, the story itself can shift dramatically.

Advancement in Brahmacharya

As I progressed, the practice expanded to include effort to remain continuous in my Ideal in all areas of experience. This was far beyond the early stages which consisted of redirecting the mind to be abstinent from thoughts and acts pertaining to intimate relations. These seemed to mirror an awakening of consciousness in the three states of awareness. In the waking state, I developed a habit of frequent analysis of my thoughts and actions by asking whether they were in line with and beneficial to my spiritual path. I gained an increased ability to control all of my senses. This expanded discipline led to the exercise of discriminative restraint even in the dream state. One gains the ability to actually recognize and dissolve dreams that are incongruent with the practice. To be specific, I could immediately dissolve sexual experiences appearing in dream state. It was not a fear-based act like one waking themselves from a nightmare mistaken to be real, but rather a conscious exertion of will to control mental projections. These advances provided experiential conviction regarding how the waking and dream state are connected. The trend of increased awareness in the three states continued as I witnessed on one occasion the progressive dissolution of the dream elements (*tanmatras*) and dream senses (*jnanendriyas*). Thus we can see that *brahmacharya*, when practiced with a mind exposed to the wisdom teachings of Vedanta via a qualified teacher, progresses from a basic purificatory exercise to understanding that there is one Self that is present in all three states of awareness. This latter cognition leans toward the higher conception of *brahmacharya* as dwelling in Brahman.

Reflections, Fruits, and Further Insights

In looking back on the first two years of my continuing vow, many other interesting insights are worth noting. First, I observed how the control of and detachment from desire has many stages and dynamics. Taking to task and prohibiting satisfaction of a deep-rooted desire such as those for sexual relations causes the mind, more specifically its ego component (*ahamkara*), to do everything in its power to suggest fulfilling that desire. These experiences can be very strong and almost feel like a mental hurricane or attack by one's own mind. When these karmas arise in the mind field one should be prepared to practice forbearance, recall the lives and qualities of spiritual exemplars who underwent similar disciplines, and remember the Lord. I found that frequently engaging the body, mind, and senses in spiritual disciplines such as *japa* (recitation of the Lord's Name), meditation, and especially religious service of the teacher and devotees, greatly diminishes these sufferings.

This routine of *sadhana* led to less intense but more frequent poking-types of suggestions from the mind. I found that a simple redirection of thought was the key technique to handling this distraction. If I neglected to do this, stronger arisings, like those previously described, would eventually happen. As one becomes adept at dispatching the more mild suggestions, one develops a concentration of mind that has a disintegrative effect on desire-

> "I realized the mind works in an analogous fashion. Specifically, I developed the ability to recognize when the mind would vibrate it such a way that a sexual thought would arise soon. Then I could dissolve these thoughts before they ever took form. To illustrate, consider a magic pool of water that if disturbed would reveal some type of image. But a skilled magician could stop the pool from vibrating before the image shows. Restraint of the mind develops similarly for the practitioner."

based *vrittis* as they arise. In my own case, I found that if I stopped resisting the desires as they suggested themselves, and rather concentrated on them with complete focus, acceptance, and freedom from self-judgement and ridicule, they would simply vanish.

After some months of further practice and recurring time with my spiritual role models, I began to observe periods of the outright absence of any suggestions to fulfill intimate desires. After decades of being immersed in desire, this was a breath of fresh air. This has to be experienced to begin to appreciate and understand the dearness that the sages and seers express for *brahmacharya*.

A second insight was clearly realizing the difference between the Self and *ahamkara*. This word, *ahamkara*, is often translated as "separate I-maker." The scriptures teach that ego expresses itself through the misuse of the senses. I noticed how my sense of individuality, with its self-centered agenda, would increase if I engaged in various sense pleasures without accompanying discrimination. The more these appetites were controlled and moderated, the more pure the mind would become in terms of keeping thoughts and actions in accordance with spiritual teachings. Hence, I learned the connection between sense control and ripening the ego so that it becomes a mechanism for revelation of Truth.

A third realization pertained to developing increasingly finer awareness of the mind and its relationship with AUM, the primeval Word. The wisdom scriptures teach that when AUM manifests various levels of the cosmic projection from causal to subtle to gross, it does so by first projecting a space (akasha) for thoughts and objects to appear. The objects then materialize out of a seed form. From my brahmacharya practice, I realized the mind works in an analogous fashion. Specifically, I developed the ability to recognize when the mind would vibrate it such a way that a sexual thought would arise soon. Then I could dissolve these thoughts before they ever took form.

To illustrate, consider a magic pool of water that if disturbed would reveal some type of image. But a skilled magician could stop the pool from vibrating before the image shows. Restraint of the mind develops similarly for the practitioner. It follows that these experiences proved to me that the mind operates much like a tiny version of AUM in how in manifests thoughts by first creating a space for them.

A final insight is that my experience with *brahmacharya* verifies many of the teachings about refinement of *prana*, raising *kundalini* to higher centers, and how this practice strengthens the mental faculty. The reader can study the wisdom chart following this article for details on this process. My mind increased its retentive capacity and ability to understand and concentrate on spiritual teachings. By simply not thinking of food and procreation while performing regular *sadhana*, my mind tended to dwell more frequently on spiritual subjects, a sign of *kundalini* rising above the three lower centers. I began to think of the my own body as an instrument for worship of God and spiritual realization, rather than a tool for pleasure/pain. With this shift, I started looking at others, especially women, as noble human beings capable of union with Reality, rather than personalities and objects for sense gratification.

Conclusion

This article is intended to illustrate how *brahmacharya*, while beginning as a simple exercise of self-control, leads to purification on increasingly subtle levels of being and development of Witness Consciousness. For maximum progress, the practitioner would do well to have a spiritual support structure consisting of a qualified teacher and holy company. This practice, if adhered to earnestly and sincerely, greatly neutralizes the effects of past conditionings. Western aspirants, with their conditionings for enjoyment and sensual excess, would do well to take up a temporary vow of *brahmacharya* and accelerate, as it were, the inner journey towards the goal of human existence.

Brother Tadrupa Josh McDaniel is an initiated student of SRV Associations. He has studied with Babaji Bob Kindler for six years. Tadrupa serves as an advisor to the SRV Board of Directors and helps assist with various activities such as classes and retreats. In his professional life, Tadrupa enjoys serving students as a college math instructor.

Reverend Chris Von Lobedon ♦

INTERFAITH REFLECTIONS
and a Personal World View

In the constant search for peaceful and beneficial relations and relationships in the world today, the ideal of the harmony of religions and religious views plays an essential part. Whether sought and practiced in the consecrated atmosphere of Church, Temple, or Mosque, pursued in the competitive fields of proliferating human activity, or discovered personally in the more confined areas of today's corrective institutions, true religion always contributes the highest and best to the lives of the people. To keep and maintain it at the level of integrity and noncompromise, however, is always the challenge, and to meet it, the individual, the organization, and the tradition must hold the twin ideal of fealty to one's personal path and honor to all other religious views. This is the intrinsic goodness that will win hearts over to God. As Swami Vivekananda has stated: *"We must all go from good, to better, to best."*

I recently observed a presentation offered by the SRV Associations at the Shutter Creek Correctional Institution. I serve the population at SCCI, and the volunteers that represent any number of traditions as a Chaplain. The currency of my work as a Chaplain is religious narratives and religious world views. The opportunity to engage the teaching of the SRV Associates at SCCI gave rise to a productive conversation about differing religious world views, duality, and non-dual truth. As much as I value religious ideas and universal religious ideas, I would like to advance a conversation about the nature of experience while trying to limit the use of religious formulations.

I propose that paradox and dualities are foundational to experience. Each person or thing is manifest as distinct and unique. My perspective on universal non-dual truth has to be reconcilable to the context of the specifics of time and place.

The presentation was offered within the rather ahistorical context of the West Coast of the United States. I say "ahistorical" because most of the inmate audience at the prison that evening were genuine products of a secular age, and had rejected the Biblical or Christian world view as being morally coercive and scientifically naïve. Some were very much aware of how addictive processes run riot in their lives. Traumatic past experiences and thought forms of destructive events are very common in prison populations. The hope for insight into the sources of their *karmic* mayhem heightened the urgency for some that attended. Many who gathered that night to hear the *Vedanta* presentation by Babaji Bob Kindler had been introduced to Transcendental Meditation (T.M.) earlier, and were inquisitive about the changes they had been experiencing through this popular form of meditation practice.

To say that twenty inmates gathered to attend a "Lecture" that night sells short both what was offered at the presentation, and what was anticipated by the audience. The *guru* of the SRV Association taught from the praxis of demonstrating *Vedanta*. I often use the term "witness" to recognize this form of integrity. The inmates attended eager to better understand the *Vedantic* teaching of *Karma Yoga*, and how *Karma* functions with regard to themselves. The audience's fidelity to self-understanding and personal growth was mutually rewarding.

One of my roles as a Chaplain is to foster this type of encounter. Interfaith reflection is very much a part of my training, and I have found it to be of valuable effect in prison Chaplaincy. The value lies in critical reflection provoked by different religious world views. The effect can be greater objectivity concerning a personal world view, a more intentional capacity for religious practice, and better awareness of the cultural or historical influences of religious understanding.

All of us have intellectual, religious, and cultural influences that I believe develop into our personal world view. The idea of developing a perspective that reflects our time and place in history is posited in the idea of individuation. We are in a time of history when Eastern religious ideas have become ubiquitous in the West. Ideas like *karma* or practices like *yoga* are available throughout the ordinary parochial culture of the United States. As a Chaplain, a working vocabulary in different faith traditions has become essential to adequately deal with the needs of the prison population. But I would offer my observations about the nature of the religious quest not by way of apology for my faith tradition, or by a form of syncretism, but instead from an experiential or phenomenological perspective.

Aspects of My Personal World View

The self-negation of the Kyoto school philosophy and detachment as articulated by Meister Eckhart are intrinsic to my world view and experience. The formation of my religious world view began with a reading list provided by John Bruce, a professor at the College of Marin. The many classics of Christian mysticism and several anthologies were all available at the public library. I read them over the course of a Summer, and upon my return in the Fall, John seemed very intrigued that I got through the list and was eager for more. John had firsthand experience of the materials he directed me to study through an epiphany, or *samadhi* experience. His experience of

Meister Eckhart

> "One of my roles as a Chaplain is to foster this type of encounter. Interfaith reflection is very much a part of my training, and I have found it to be of valuable effect in prison Chaplaincy. The value lies in critical reflection provoked by different religious world views. The effect can be greater objectivity concerning a personal world view, a more intentional capacity for religious practice, and better awareness of the cultural or historical influences of religious understanding."

"Nothingness" provided him the spiritual name of Zero. After several years John introduced me to his wife, and they brought me into their lives. My early training was pragmatic in the sense of all being reconcilable to his experience of "Nothingness."

John was cautious in his approach to directing my studies, but slowly introduced me to Eastern thinking. This salted my understanding of Western mysticism. He also introduced me to the Presbyterian Church. I was a welder and tradesman in the marine industry, but eventually switched my academic emphasis from the sciences to the arts and pursued a career in the church through training at San Francisco Theological Seminary. There I worked my way through the standard theological curriculum with the intent of becoming a Minister. Dr. Roy Fairchild introduced me to the work C. G. Jung, and Masao Abe introduced me to Nishida Kitaro and the Kyoto School philosophy. These sources and others that remain unmentioned have become amalgamated into what I am referring to as my world view.

In attempting to give expression to my world view, I do so with the specifics of a time and place to explain it in a way that does not rely too heavily upon dogma or religious narratives. "Transpersonal center," "that which is beyond us," "a higher power," all represent an attempt to acknowledge that which I identify as God. Religious narratives help to explain how consciousness functions through metaphors, or analogies and symbols. Therefore, the cosmology offered in, say, Hinduism, has an impact on how individuals perceive themselves, but is not to be taken any more or less literally than a Christian or Biblical narrative world view. There are merits to either narrative world view, and being acquainted with both may enhance an individual's understanding of either one. Depth psychology, Jungian or archetypal psychology, has influenced my understanding in this regard.

It takes an Ego to Lose an Ego

To me, right intention is very closely tied to an ego structure and the purposes a person serves. Goodness is unavoidable in seeking spiritual attainment. I would also contend that kenosis, "immediate experience," or élan vital, is the experiential foundation of allowing that goodness to be expressed. A foundation of ego development needs to be established to reduce instinctive and selfish tendencies. I am fond of the saying, "it takes an ego to lose an ego." I propose a person needs to become accomplished in the sense of using their personal life experience in service to greater purposes commonly identified as good, commendable, or even virtuous — in other words, to be able to serve God. Reciprocity between the uniquely individual and the universal of serving God reflects a paradox in the expression of our will. In a similar way, "it takes a will to lose the will." The will that is in service of the ego is abrogated in service to God. Compassion and goodwill is the product of relinquishing forms of self-will through kenosis in service to "that which is greater than ourselves."

Within the context of prison chaplaincy, and in general religious expression, there are mixed motives in spiritual aspiration. For example, some of the inmates in attendance at the *Vedanta* event that evening sought to refine a spirituality better adapted to affect their unripe will than a capacity of service to goodness. Without service to God, the likely result is a type of hubris, or in Jungian terms, "inflation." Types of magical thinking that would attempt to bend the universe to our wills is common to many forms of religious and secular endeavor. This is in service to the ego and not necessarily bad in itself, but it is not the nature of religious experience founded on self-emptying. Goodness is unavoidable in seeking and attaining spiritual maturity.

Purpose is an expression of intent. Intent is therefore a function of the will and is refined or guided in response to our world view. It is also an expression of our history and the events that have defined our existence. Part of my high regard for the *Vedanta* and the SRV teachers that visited us that evening comes from recognizing their desire to teach and inspire, and to offer themselves in service of others. This is a form of goodness, and a characteristic of the intent that I value as Chaplain. It is the nature of a vocation or a calling in my tradition. Each of us has a unique form of self-expression that is nurtured through religious practice. The characteristic that differentiates religious self-expression is points of reference that transcend and abrogate our self-will. This is a form of paradox or duality that is distinctly religious and reciprocal in nature.

I encourage those incarcerated at SCCI to use their life experience in service to others. Investment in recovery, mentoring, religious community, and nurturing the vulnerable allows redemptive purpose to emerge from destructive past experiences. Incorporating past experience is an expression of integrity and individuation. We are distinct individuals, but also give expression to principles that are collective in the sense of being good. To advance understanding and be faithful to my office is natural to me and the self-expression of the culmination of my life experience. To be a person existing in a time and place, and to serve a particular end, is a foundation of experience that I resist leaving behind to discuss theory.

> "Types of magical thinking that would attempt to bend the universe to our wills is common to many forms of religious and secular endeavor. This is in service to the ego and not necessarily bad in itself, but it is not the nature of religious experience founded on self-emptying. Goodness is unavoidable in seeking and attaining spiritual maturity."

Mitigating Contrasting Religious Narratives

If thought of on a spectrum, literalism and syncretism appear as a polemic. Many forms of polemic organize as functions of duality. A rigid literalism on one end makes it impossible to reconcile contrasting world views. Utilizing such narratives to better understand the nature of being in terms of philosophy or phenomenology mitigates contradicting religious narratives. The extraction of meaning and the praxis of being faithful are transformative effects that result from reflection on religious narratives. This process affects an individual's identity and purpose. For example, my identity as a Chaplain, a Presbyterian minister, and a Christian, all function to inform and guide my self-expression. My purpose is reciprocal in the sense of being expressed in the mundane activities of daily living and the sublime in religious aspiration. This poses another form of duality that is intrinsic to religious experience.

Beneficial Duality and Unifying Nonduality

After the presentation of *Vedanta* and *Karma Yoga* that evening, we all reflected on the outcome and realized that the dialogue around our unique perspectives on faith and practice could be productive to develop further. We do have some contrasting approaches and primary sources of our religious understanding. However, the solidarity of spirit and shared aspiration of service is a form of non-dual truth. To quote a volunteer from the prison who was present that evening, "Some people seek to serve God, and others seek for God to serve them." In the service to God, all are one. Paradoxically, this Oneness is expressed in dualities.

Reverend Chris von Lobedan has served Shutter Creek Correctional Institution in Coos Bay Oregon for 17 years. His Doctor of Ministry and Master of Divinity were awarded from San Francisco Theological Seminary. He was the pastor of the First Presbyterian Church of Coos Bay for 13 years. He was recognized with the Transitional Services Employee of the Year award for his work in the religious reentry program Home for Good. He has worked extensively inside his institution to train volunteers to understand the importance of assisting those with whom they work with faith-based assistance as they transition from prison. He has brought a specific faith-traditions approach to that training and been one of the leaders in the development of Home for Good.

Some Essential Quotes of Meister Eckhart

"Through the higher love the whole life of man is to be elevated from temporal selfishness to the spring of all love, to God: man will again be master over nature by abiding in God and lifting her up to God."

"The most powerful prayer, one wellnigh omnipotent, and the worthiest work of all is the outcome of a quiet mind. The quieter it is the more powerful, the worthier, the deeper, the more telling and more perfect the prayer is. To the quiet mind all things are possible. What is a quiet mind? A quiet mind is one which nothing weighs on, nothing worries, which, free from ties and from all self-seeking, is wholly merged into the will of God and dead to its own."

"….we should know the judgments of God. ….we should know the Godhead which has flowed into the Father and filled Him with joy, and which has flowed into the Son and filled Him with wisdom, and that the Two are essentially One."

"As the peculiar faculty of the eye is to see form and color, and of the ear to hear sweet tones and voices, so is aspiration peculiar to the soul. To relax from ceaseless aspiration is sin. This energy of aspiration directed to and grasping God, as far as is possible for the creature, is a divine virtue. Through this faculty the soul acquires such great confidence that she deems nothing in the Divine Nature beyond her reach."

"All that the Eternal Father teaches and reveals is His being, His nature, and His Godhead, which He manifests to us in His Son, and teaches us that we are also His Son."

German Philosopher born on December 30, 1260, Eckhart von Hochheim O.P., commonly known as Meister Eckhart, was a German theologian, philosopher and mystic, born near Gotha, in the Landgraviate of Thuringia in the Holy Roman Empire.

Live-Streaming Class Series from SRV Hawaii for 2019

▪ Obstacles & Progress in Spiritual Life & Practice
Dec. 30, Jan 6, 13, 20, & 27th, 2018/19

Spiritual success concerns subtleties that one cannot smell, taste, touch, see, and hear with the five senses, but its failure has more to do with what one did with the five senses in the past, and the karma one created with them — both in the present lifetime, and in past existences. Tracing the cause of karma and its resultant sufferings (and enjoyments) is the crying need of the spiritually ignorant person, the greatest challenge for the aspirant on the spiritual path, and a source of peace for the adept and luminary who masters the process. These luminaries state that progress along the spiritual path is rare, as are the requisites which make it possible. They also communicate that even a small amount of headway by the aspirant in any given lifetime amounts to a substantial attainment overall.

▪ God/Brahman Reflected in the Universe
March 10 & 17, 2019

The profound and exceptional axiom called Chidabhasa in Vedanta is unique to world philosophy. Unanswered questions concerning the presence of Divine Reality in the world have gone unresolved by Western philosophers for centuries, they, never reaching a conclusion or finding a sensible solution. In Mother India, however, the insight of "reflected consciousness," perceived early on, has put an end to such unnecessary queries and futile intellectual wanderings. As the moon shines by borrowed light, so too does all of Nature reflect Nondual Awareness, while leaving Ultimate Reality completely untouched, unchanged, and ever-abiding in Its own transcendental Essence.

▪ Your Subtle Body: Mind as the "Kingdom of Heaven" Within
April 7, 14, 21, & 28th, 2019

Where is the Kingdom of Heaven that lies within mentioned by Jesus, or the akashas revealed by the Indian seers, or the lokas espied by the yogis, or the bardos seen and explored by the luminaries of Tibetan Buddhism? They are certainly not up in the sky, or somewhere inside the physical body. They all lie within the mind, called the subtle body, or "sukshma sharira," in Vedanta. These realms are seen by living beings in the dream state, but are not engaged consciously, leaving humanity with the impression that dreams are figments of the imagination rather than experiences occurring at different levels of awareness. Changing this misconception is a key to inner life. The mind is not the brain; it contains all the kingdoms of Heaven within.

▪ Proofs of Truth in Advaita Vedanta
June 9, 16, 23, & 30th, 2019

Scarcely considered in educational systems or philosophical circles of today are the Six Proofs of Reality in Advaita Vedanta, securely posited by Vedic seers over millennia. India's Vaisisheka Darshana also offers up six more proofs, and India's Puranas add two more into that convincing stock. Sankhya Yoga contributes the Six Proofs of Purusha. Verbal testimony, analogy, inference, similitude, presumption, direct perception, nonapprehension, traditional hearsay, witness consciousness — all of these and more deserve inspection and contemplation by the ardent seeker searching for the truth of Divine Reality.

▪ Rebirth, Reincarnation, & The Illusion of Death
August 11, 18, & 25th, 2019

The very presence of the desire for freedom in the mind and the ability to willfully detach from all things earthly suggests that the human soul has as its natural and abiding condition the state of boundlessness and eternity. Add to this the existence of the mind's memory of everything from past lifetimes to accurate visions of the future, and the matter comes to a rest. Death is an outright illusion. The unoriginated nature of the Soul, Atman, sheds the notion of beginnings and endings as easily as a duck's feathers repel water. This fact reveals another salient fact for the sincere spiritual aspirant to recognize, that life is dreamlike, and that birth and death take place only in Nature, not in the Soul. According to the mind's quality of mental projections, all based in actions perpetrated prior to birth and mental impressions formed in past lifetimes, the incarnating being takes recourse to a long, arduous, and sometimes endless series of bodily existences in ignorance of its blissful, changeless Essence.

Live-Streaming Class Series, Continued

▪ Kundalini Yoga as Mahayoga
September 8, 15, & 22nd, 2019

The most highly realized and enlightened souls tell of two prominent yogas among the many yogas available to benefit the spiritual aspirant's practice and progress. These two yogas are of the nondual type, actually transcending the need for any type of practice based upon attainment, and replacing that with the smooth and natural facility of abiding in Yoga. These two yogas, termed Abhavayoga and Mahayoga, are intrinsically connected with the two modes of Awareness called "Emptiness" and "Fullness," the former founded in the welcome absence of all name and form in transcendent indivisibility and the latter realizing all of that, but embracing both form and formlessness in comprehensive Oneness.

▪ Ma Kali, The Adhyashakti
October 27th, November 3rd, 2019

Imminent on the world scene in this day and age, and deeply involved in the lives and aspirations of Her deeply dedicated devotees, Divine Mother Kali nevertheless remains mostly unknown to a greater percentage of embodied beings on earth, and also a complete enigma to those who have begun to hear of Her. Described as the Adhyashakti in revealed scriptures, and as the original, preeminent Feminine Force, She is the one, indivisible, transcendent, primal Being whose supremely Self-willed nature guides and oversees the functions of all the worlds, as well as the many beings occupying them. As the great Sannyasin, Swami Vivekananda, has stated about Her, "She is my especial thing." Also, "May She, the Primal Guide, my refuge be....."

▪ The New Religion of This Age:
Swami Vivekananda's Four Yogas
November 17, 24th, 2019

Expertly and efficaciously blending ignorance-destroying wisdom with heartfelt devotion for God with form, while simultaneously mingling in the subtle spiritual art of deep and intensely centered meditation on formless Reality — all followed up and woven together with dharmic activities focused around selfless service of God in mankind — all this would equal the sweet and powerful coalescence of what has been termed by sages and seers as Integral Yoga, Purna Yoga, or the Synthesis of Yoga. The result, according to Swami Vivekananda, would be the ideal and multidimensional spiritual being of the present age, eclipsing the practitioner of the past who was, perhaps, adept at only one or two of these four yogas, at best.

▪ Knowledge & Its Stages
December 22nd, 29th, 2019

The ancient and well-thought system of India's Seven Stages of Knowledge, and the Fourteen Stages of Upper and Lower Knowledge, open up new and deep dimensions for any aspirant of Truth who wishes to consummate a fuller understanding around this important subject. Not only does this fine blend of spiritual and philosophical insight introduce the student and seeker to upper echelons of the mind's otherwise uncharted Awareness, it also describes in great detail just how the benighted soul, laboring under the regime of root ignorance, rises up and out of such heavy mental confines to recognize both the ultimate Goal of innate Freedom, and the infinite potential it has in gaining Enlightenment via higher Knowledge.

* Livestream.com/Babaji Bob Kindler

SRV Vedanta Associations — Babaji's Teaching Schedule, 2019

SRV Hawai'i Administrative Office
PO Box 1364
Honoka'a, HI 96727

SRV Associations' website: www.srv.org
email: srvinfo@srv.org
Phone: 808-990-3354

SRV Oregon
1922 SE 42nd Ave.,
Portland, OR 97215
Ph: 503-774-2410

SRV San Francisco
465 Brussels Street
San Francisco, CA 94134
Ph: 415-468-4680

February, 2019

SRV San Francisco
2/9 Sat 6:00pm **Sarasvati Puja**
2/10 Sun 9:30am Class: Tejabindu Upanisad

SRV Oregon (Call for meditation times)
2/13 Wed 7:00pm Principles of the Upanisads, with Anurag
2/15 Fri 7:00pm Vedanta 101, with Annapurna Sarada
2/16 Sat 9:30am Class: Akshi Upanisad
6:00pm **Sri Ramakrishna Puja**
2/17 Sun 9:30am Class: Akshi Upanisad
2/20 Wed 7:00pm Principles of the Upanisads, with Anurag
2/21 - 2/25 SRV Winter Retreat in Oregon

SRV Winter Retreat, February 21-25, Oregon
Subject: Manasana: The Art of Mental Postures
(arrive Thursday night 21st, depart Monday 25th at noon)
For details on all retreats, see Retreat Pages

2019 SRV Hawaii Retreat #1, Spring
Big Island, Hawaii, March 21-25
Subject: Encomium & Shravana, Manana, & Nididhyasana
Teachings & Instruction on Reflection and Implementation

May, 2019

SRV San Francisco
5/11 Sat 6:00pm SRV Puja
5/12 Sun 9:30am Class: Tejabindu Upanisad

SRV Oregon (Call for meditation times)
5/15 Wed 7:00pm Principles of the Upanisads, with Anurag
5/17 Fri 7:00pm Satsang with Babaji
5/18 Sat 9:30am Class: Akshi Upanisad
6:00pm SRV Puja, Siva Puja
5/19 Sun 9:30am Class: Akshi Upanisad
5/22 Wed 7:00pm Principles of the Upanisads, with Anurag
5/23 - 5/27 Memorial Weekend Retreat

Memorial Day Weekend Retreat, May 23-27
Subject: My Guru's Teachings, 2:
Swami Aseshananda's Unique Look at Spiritual Life in America
Location: Windwood Waters (Wind River Region, WA)
(arrive Thursday evening 23rd, depart Monday 27th at noon)
For details, see Retreat Pages

Visit srv.org for all retreat details
Weekend Classes webcasted, 9:30 am to 12:30 pm, Pacific Time

July, 2019

SRV San Francisco
7/11 Thu SRV SF Summer Retreat Begins at Foresthill, CA.

SRV American River Retreat over Guru Purnima
July 11th -15th, Foresthill, CA
Subject: Maintaining Spirituality and Peace of Mind
While Fulfilling Duties in the World
Plus: Chanting, Memorization, & Discourse on selected Stotrams
(arrive Thursday 11th, depart Monday 15th, noon)

SRV Oregon (Call for meditation times)
7/17 Wed 7:00pm Principles of the Upanisads, with Anurag
7/19 Fri 7:00pm Satsang with Babaji
7/20 Sat 9:30am Class: Akshi Upanisad
6:00pm SRV Puja, Siva Puja
7/21 Sun 9:30am Class: Akshi Upanisad
7/24 Wed 7:00pm Vedanta 101, with Annapurna Sarada
7/26 Fri 6:00pm Open Seminar Satsang with Babaji
7/26-28 Weekend Seminar

SRV Weekend Seminar with Satsang, July 26-28
Subject: Jnanamritam Chalisa – "Like The Sky" Stotram, II
2 classes Sat., 2 classes Sun.
More Singing, Discourse, Commentary, & Contemplation
on these 40 verses from the Avadhuta Gita

October, 2019

SRV San Francisco
10/5 Sat 6:00pm Divine Mother/SRV Puja
10/6 Sun 9:30am Class: Tejabindu Upanisad

SRV Oregon (Call for meditation times)
10/9 Wed 7:00pm Principles of the Upanisads, with Anurag
10/10 - 10/14 SRV Fall Retreat, Discoverer's Day

SRV Fall Retreat, October 10-14 Location: TBA
Subject: The Seven Goddess Upanisads (Continued)
Tripura Sundari Upanisad (& conclusion of Yogakundalini)
(arrive Thursday evening 10th, depart Monday 14th at noon)

10/16 Wed 7:00pm Vedanta 101, with Annapurna Sarada
10/19 Sat 9:30am Class: Akshi Upanisad
6:00pm **Sri Durga Devi Puja**
10/20 Sun 9:30am Class: Akshi Upanisad

2019 SRV Hawaii Retreat #2, Winter
Big Island, Hawaii, November 8-12
Subject: Comprehensive Teachings Around AUM, The Word

Announcing SRV India Pilgrimage 2019, November 27 - December 11th
Destinations: Delhi, Kolkata, Chennai Limited Space, Advance Confirmation Advised (babaji@hialoha.net)

SRV Vedanta Associations — Babaji's Teaching Schedule, 2019
SRV Hawai'i Retreat Center & Ashram

Hawaii Spring Retreat: Reintroducing The Encomium
Title: Shravana, Manana, & Nididhyasana
Location: Paauilo, Big Island of Hawaii
March 21st - 25th, 2019

Sunday Live Streaming Classes, 2:30 - 5:30pm
Hawai'i SRV Ashram   Directions: Call: 808-990-3354

- **Obstacles & Progress in Spiritual Life & Prac.**
  Dec. 30, Jan 6, 13, 20, 27th, 2018/19
- **God/Brahman Reflected in the Universe**
  March, 10, 17, 2019
- **Your Subtle Body: Mind as the "Kingdom of Heaven" Within**
  April 7, 14, 21, & 28th, 2019
- **Proofs of Truth in Advaita Vedanta**
  June 9, 16, 23, & 30th, 2019
- **Rebirth & Reincarnation: The Illusion of Death**
  August 11, 18, & 25th, 2019
- **Kundalini Yoga as Mahayoga**
  September 8, 15, & 22nd, 2019
- **Ma Kali, The Adhyashakti**
  October 27th, November 3rd, 2019
- **The New Religion of This Age: Swami Vivekananda's Four Yogas**
  November 17, 24th, 2019
- **Knowledge & Its Stages**
  December 22nd, 29th, 2019

Hawaii Winter Retreat
Title: Comprehensive Teachings on AUM, The Word
Location: Paauilo, Big Island of Hawaii
November 8th - 12st, 2019

Also, check www.srv.org for Hawaii retreats or see our Retreats Pages in the back of this issue
Sign up for:
- SRV Magazine: Nectar of Non-Dual Truth
- Raja Yoga email study with Babaji
- SRV's Facebook page
- SRV's YouTube channel: Teaching videos

SRV Hawai'i Administrative Office:
PO Box 1364
Honoka'a, HI 96727
Ph: 808-990-3354

SRV Associations' website:
www.srv.org
email:
srvinfo@srv.org

See our SRV Facebook Page   facebook.com/srv.vedanta

SRV Vedanta Associations Website
www.srv.org
srvinfo@srv.org

SRV On The Web
Visit www.srv.org to find:
- SRV's Livestream Channel
- Webcast Time Zone Schedule

SRV's YouTube Channel Class Series
- Advaita of the Avatars
- Devotion of Nonseparation
- The Wisdom Particle
- Non-Touch Yoga
- Mahamudra & Tibetan Buddhism
- Shakta-Advaita-vada
- Food, Prana, & Sadhana
- Satsangs with Babaji

Explore our Website links to find:
- Sanskrit Chants to learn/practice
- Devotional Songs
- Audio Discourses

Teachings:
- Articles
- Raja Yoga Sutras Study
- SRV's Teachings for Youth/Children

Magazine:
- Order back issues of Nectar
- View our online archive of Nectar

Dharma Teachings & Sangha News
- Mundamala – SRV Sangha e-magazine
- SRV Sangha e-newsletter

Full of teachings & current events

SRV Associations — Retreats for 2019

SRV Oregon Retreat
February 21st - 25th, 2019, Oregon
Retreat Topic: *Manasana: The Art of Mental Postures*

The ability to maintain peace of mind while working in the world, in the field of action, is dependent upon being able to abide comfortably in a state of inaction, like in meditation. The state of conscious inaction is, in turn, reliant upon a control of mind that keeps it from wandering away due to modes of laziness and distraction (tamas & rajas). To ensure that the mind remains under one's control, the seers advise the practice of mental asanas, fixed postures of mind that heal, spiritualize, and eventually provide entrance into the transcendent state of Awareness, called samadhi, satori, and nirvana. Physical postures can never provide such spiritual treasure, nor can breathing exercises, spouse, offspring, or wealth, property, and fame. And in fact, these latter are often what robs people of their basic peace of mind — as is seen in today's societies and workplaces.

SRV's winter retreat in Oregon is especially designed to focus in on learning about these special positions of the mind, taking them up, practicing them, and establishing them as everyday modes of awareness — both in the world while doing duties, and in spiritual practices that help the soul to grow in its ability to know Brahman, Divine Reality.

"A positive stance, a firm resolve, unshakable perseverance, and an unwavering faith, form the crucial content of a mind that is destined for success, in whatever field of endeavor it takes up. Of all of these, the first, a positive stance, is needed the most at the very outset. In the Eightfold Path of Buddhism, which when implemented into life and practice sets the stage for spiritual advancement, it is perfect view — samyak dristi — that allows for all initial forward motion. In Patanjali's Eight-Limbed Yoga system, it is the removal of bhrantidarshana resulting in correct philosophical orientation that provides for swift and definite spiritual growth. In the Bhagavad Gita, it is the generation of a clear understanding — buddhya vishuddhaya — that sets up the necessary ability of transcendence that follows, in stages. Along the path of Bhakti Yoga, it is the clarity of mind assimilated from holy company — sadhu-satsanga — that brings increased devotion for the Ideal, called the Ishtam. Thus, a positive mental stance is crucial in life and action ...." Babaji Bob Kindler, Manasana: The Art of Mental Postures

Location: Mindful Heart Forest Retreat, Columbia River Gorge
Arrival: Thursday, February 21st, between 4 & 6pm
Departure: Monday, February 25th, at 12:00 noon
Tuition (all inclusive): $640; students $415   **Registration:** Begins now. Tuition is due by February 1st
Financial hardship? Call 808-990-3354   **Register by email:** srvinfo@srv.org or by phone 808-990-3354

SRV Spring Retreat Over Memorial Day Weekend
May 23rd – 27th, 2019, Wind River region, Stevenson, Washington
Subject: *My Guru's Teachings, 2: Swami Aseshananda's unique look at spiritual life and practice in America*

Part one of this series, given in early 2018, covered the observances of this great soul on all that took place in this country around spiritual discovery and its attempted implementation by the Western culture over some 60 years of his presence here. Part 2 continues along in this vein, while drawing in facets of the swami's own realizations as he taught amongst the Westerners who came to Vedanta and recognized it as the religion and philosophy of the Age.

Location: Windwood Waters retreat site near Stevenson, WA
Arrival: Thursday, May 23rd, by 9:00 pm **Departure:** Monday, May 27th, 12:00 noon
Tuition (all-inclusive): $690; Students:: $425
Registration: Begins now. Tuition due by May 7th
Register by email: srvinfo@srv.org or by phone 808-990-3354
Financial hardship? Call 808-990-3354

SRV American River Gurupurnima Retreat, 2019
July 11th – 15th, 2019, Foresthill, CA
Maintaining Spirituality and Peace of Mind while Fulfilling Duties in the World
* Including Chanting of Devotional Songs and Study of Dharma Teachings

Beginning with chanting of the Bhagavad Gita and early morning meditations prior to dawn, and ending each divine evening with devotional worship and Satsang at dusk, the day in between is filled with dharma classes, chanting the Names of the Lord and Mother of the Universe, recreation and lunch along the beautiful American River in the hot afternoon sun, and late afternoon question and answer sessions with the instructors. The entire event is set up to allow the aspirant to live in holy company for a few sacred days – meditating, studying, serving, and growing in the spirit. Time for silent reflection in nature and deep sleep among the peaceful regions filled with forests and birds complete the experience of this 30-year long summer retreat that SRV continues to offer to all souls interested in healing, learning, and expanding their awareness of God and Self.

Location: Private land in Foresthill, California near the American River
Arrival: Thursday, July 11th, by 9pm,
Last day of retreat: Monday, July 15th (approximately noon, clean up follows)
Tuition (all inclusive): Adults: $570, students: $345   Daily rate, $160/$100, student
Registration: Begins now. Tuition is due by June 25th
Financial hardship? Call 808-990-3354 to discuss options
Register by email: srvinfo@srv.org or by phone 808-990-3354

SRV Fall Columbus Day Retreat, 2019
October 10th – 14th, 2019, Location: TBA
Subject: *The Seven Goddess Upanisads: Part 5 — Tripura Sundari Upanisad*

In SRV's pursuit of studying all of the esoteric "Mother" Upanisads, the Tripura Sundari comes up next. Studied thus far over four Autumn retreats are the Devi Upanisad, Sita Upanisad, Saubaghya Lakshmi Upanisad, Savitri Upanisad, and the Yoga Kundalini Upanisad.

Location: TBA
Arrival: Thursday, Oct 10th, TBA
Departure: Monday, Oct 14th, 12:00 noon
Tuition: Adults: $450: Students: $225, Lodging/Meals, TBA
Registration: Begins now. Tuition by September 25th
Financial hardship? Call 808-990-3354 to discuss options
Register by email: srvinfo@srv.org or by phone 808-990-3354

SRV Summer Seminar in 2019, July 26th - 28th, Portland, Oregon, SRV Ashram
Subject: *Jnanamritam Chalisa 2 — "Like The Sky" Stotram*
Chanting, Discourse, Commentary, and Contemplation of these Forty Verses from the Avadhuta Gita

Schedule: Friday, July 26th: 6:00 PM – Satsang
Saturday, July 27th: 6:00am – 5:00pm (meditation, breakfast, morning and afternoon classes, dinner)
Sunday, July 28th: 6:00am – 5:00pm (meditation, breakfast, morning and afternoon classes)
Tuition (all-inclusive): $260; student, $130
Registration: Begins now. Tuition due by July 1st
Financial hardship? Call 808-990-3354 to discuss options
Register by email: srvinfo@srv.org or by phone 808-990-3354
Accommodations: This is a non-residential seminar
Contact us if you would like assistance with lodging, nearby. 808-990-3354 // srvinfo@srv.org

SRV Associations — Hawaii Retreat #1 for 2019

March 21st - 25th, 2019, Big Island of Hawaii   Reintroducing "The Encomium"
Retreat Topic: *Shravana, Manana, & Nididhyasana*

"The Encomium," a testament to the wonders and nobility of spiritual self-effort, is a collection of poetic verses by Babaji Bob Kindler on the many numbered systems of dharma in India. Combining these sutras under the auspice of The Three Proofs of Truth — hearing the Truth from an illumined preceptor, contemplating It in a sacred and secluded setting, and realizing It after Its superlative presence has purified and matured the mind — the ancient and time-tested methods present in the Vedanta Philosophy will find fruition in the sincere student's mind.

In this retreat, students will have the opportunity to not only focus in on the meaning and power of this indispensable tool for sadhana, but also spend measured time in all three facets of it — all under the direct supervision and counsel of the teacher. Dharma classes will be built around the active implementation of these great philosophical and spiritual practices, allowing time not only to listen and learn about their unique content, but also to enter directly into them during private and silent intervals occurring daily during the retreat.

"....suffice to say that the aspirant must first hear the truth, then roll it over in the mind for a time. The first part occurs in the presence of the spiritual preceptor, or at least this is the best and classic way. The second act marks the difference between contemplation and meditation, the former dealing with and operating at the level of conceptualizations and the latter being utilized more for communion with the Deity and Formless Brahman. After these two have been implemented, realization, or direct spiritual experience, should be the result. No doubt, fear, or lack of clarity can persist in the atmosphere of the well-guided, well-activated triputi of the Three Potent Practices or Three Proofs of Truth."   Footfalls of the Indian Rishis, Babaji Bob Kindler

Location: SRV Retreat Center on the Hamakua Coast, Big Island of Hawaii
Arrival: Thursday, March 21st, between 4 & 6pm
Departure: Monday, March 25th, at 12:00 noon
Tuition, Meals, & Lodging: Shared rooms, $515/person; Private room, $565; Tenting, $415-465/person
Registration: Begins now. Tuition is due by March 7th
Register by email: srvinfo@srv.org or by phone 808-990-3354
Financial hardship? Contact us to learn about options

SRV Associations — Hawaii Retreat #2 for 2019

November 8th - 12th, 2019, Big Island of Hawaii
Retreat Topic: Comprehensive *Teachings on AUM, The Word*

"In the beginning was the Word, and the Word was with God, and the Word was God." John, 1:1

Of all the lost lore of true religion and authentic philosophy in this present age of spiritual ignorance, perhaps the most lamentable of disappearances are the many clarifying truths around The Word, spoken of in Sanskrit as AUM. Even two thousand years ago, in the time of the great soul, Lord Jesus, knowledge about The Word's deeper ramifications had gone missing in the minds of the people of that day and time. Five hundred and fifty years before Jesus, the incomparable soul, Lord Buddha, saw its powerful teachings being covered over by habitual worship of the ancestors and other less potent practices and insights, saying: *"For, whoso quells desire, gains expertise in etymology and terminology, and comes to know the deep meanings in words and letters, he is a great soul. He bears the physical body for the last time."*

Facets of The Word's significance such as waking, dreaming, and deep sleep, Nonorigination, and The Secret of Creation will be explored in depth in this fascinating and engaging retreat held on the Big Island of Hawaii.

Location: Hamakua, Big Island of Hawaii   **Arrival:** Friday, November 8th, between 4 & 6pm
Departure: Tuesday, November 12th, at 12:00 noon
Tuition, Meals, & Lodging: Shared rooms, $515/person; Private room, $565; Tenting, $415-465/person
Registration: Begins now. Tuition is due by October 20th
Register by email: srvinfo@srv.org or by phone 808-990-3354   **Financial hardship?** Contact us to learn options

Donation/Order Form
Suggested donation $15 per issue

Nectar #35 is available for free if you write, email, or call for a copy by January 15, 2020.
Your generous donations make Nectar available to others.
Those who donate $15 or more for the next issue will be added our subscribers list.

☐ Please send me/my friend a free copy of the next issue of Nectar.
☐ Send me ____ copies to give to friends, Spiritual Centers, or a business of my choice. (fill out back of form)
☐ I want to make sure there are future issues of Nectar ($200 and up)

Nectar needs sustaining donors! ($500 and up) Your gift is tax-deductible.

Please fill out the back side of this form and mail it with your check to:
SRV Associations, PO Box 1364, Honokaa, HI 96727
MasterCard or Visa accepted • Make checks payable to: SRV Associations
808-990-3354 • srvinfo@srv.org • www.srv.org   #34

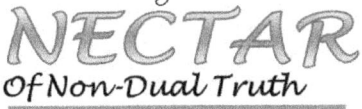

Donation/Order Form
Suggested donation $15 per issue

Nectar #35 is available for free if you write, email, or call for a copy by January 15, 2020.
Your generous donations make Nectar available to others.
Those who donate $15 or more for the next issue will be added our subscribers list.

☐ Please send me/my friend a free copy of the next issue of Nectar.
☐ Send me ____ copies to give to friends, Spiritual Centers, or a business of my choice. (fill out back of form)
☐ I want to make sure there are future issues of Nectar ($200 and up)

Nectar needs sustaining donors! ($500 and up) Your gift is tax-deductible.

Please fill out the back side of this form and mail it with your check to:
SRV Associations, PO Box 1364, Honokaa, HI 96727
MasterCard or Visa accepted • Make checks payable to: SRV Associations
808-990-3354 • srvinfo@srv.org • www.srv.org   #34

Donation/Order Form
Suggested donation $15 per issue

Nectar #35 is available for free if you write, email, or call for a copy by January 15, 2020.
Your generous donations make Nectar available to others.
Those who donate $15 or more for the next issue will be added our subscribers list.

☐ Please send me/my friend a free copy of the next issue of Nectar.
☐ Send me ____ copies to give to friends, Spiritual Centers, or a business of my choice. (fill out back of form)
☐ I want to make sure there are future issues of Nectar ($200 and up)

Nectar needs sustaining donors! ($500 and up) Your gift is tax-deductible.

Please fill out the back side of this form and mail it with your check to:
SRV Associations, PO Box 1364, Honokaa, HI 96727
MasterCard or Visa accepted • Make checks payable to: SRV Associations
808-990-3354 • srvinfo@srv.org • www.srv.org   #34

Your Information:

Name: _____
Address: _____
City, State, Zip: _____
Email: _____

Additional Address: (please use a sheet of paper for more addresses)

Name: _____
Address: _____
City, State, Zip: _____
Email: _____

Do you wish to pay by Mastercard or Visa?
Card No.: _____ Amount: _____
Exp. date: _____ Phone no.: _____
Signature: _____

Questions? call SRV Associations: 808-990-3354

- -

Your Information:

Name: _____
Address: _____
City, State, Zip: _____
Email: _____

Additional Address: (please use a sheet of paper for more addresses)

Name: _____
Address: _____
City, State, Zip: _____
Email: _____

Do you wish to pay by Mastercard or Visa?
Card No.: _____ Amount: _____
Exp. date: _____ Phone no.: _____
Signature: _____

Questions? call SRV Associations: 808-990-3354

- -

Your Information:

Name: _____
Address: _____
City, State, Zip: _____
Email: _____

Additional Address: (please use a sheet of paper for more addresses)

Name: _____
Address: _____
City, State, Zip: _____
Email: _____

Do you wish to pay by Mastercard or Visa?
Card No.: _____ Amount: _____
Exp. date: _____ Phone no.: _____
Signature: _____

Questions? call SRV Associations: 808-990-3354

www.ingramcontent.com/pod-product-compliance
Lightning Source LLC
Chambersburg PA
CBHW080024110526
44587CB00021BA/3839